The Lone Wolf's Way of Solitude

Reawaken Your Creativity, Confidence, Leadership, and Purpose Through a Strong Individualist Lifestyle

David J. Polak

© **Copyright 2022 - All rights reserved.**

The content contained within this book may not be reproduced, duplicated or transmitted without direct written permission from the author or the publisher.

Under no circumstances will any blame or legal responsibility be held against the publisher, or author, for any damages, reparation, or monetary loss due to the information contained within this book, either directly or indirectly.

Legal Notice:

This book is copyright protected. It is only for personal use. You cannot amend, distribute, sell, use, quote or paraphrase any part, or the content within this book, without the consent of the author or publisher.

Disclaimer Notice:

Please note the information contained within this document is for educational and entertainment purposes only. All effort has been executed to present accurate, up to date, reliable, complete information. No warranties of any kind are declared or implied. Readers acknowledge that the author is not engaged in the rendering of legal, financial, medical or professional advice. The content within this book has been derived from various sources. Please consult a licensed professional before attempting any techniques outlined in this book.

By reading this document, the reader agrees that under no circumstances is the author responsible for any losses, direct or indirect, that are incurred as a result of the use of the information contained within this document, including, but not limited to, errors, omissions, or inaccuracies.

Table of Contents

INTRODUCTION 8
   THE NATURE OF WOLVES AND THAT OF HUMANS 10
   YOU, YOUR SOLITUDE, AND THIS BOOK 12
   MY OWN JOURNEY 14
   ALONE IN GOOD COMPANY 16

CHAPTER 1: THE CALL FOR SOLITUDE—THE FIRST STEP OF A LONE WOLF 18
   MISCONCEPTIONS ABOUT SOLITUDE AND THE LONE WOLF LIFESTYLE.. 19
      Solitude Is Total Self-Isolation 21
      Solitary People Never Want to Make Friends 22
      Solitary People Are Antisocial 23
      Solitary People Are Socially Inept 24
      Solitary People Are Lazy 24
      Solitary People Have a Superiority Complex 25
   LONELINESS AND ALONENESS 27
      Loneliness 27
      Aloneliness 29
   SOLITUDE 29
   THE BENEFITS OF SOLITUDE FOR EXTROVERTS 31
   SOLITUDE AS REBELLION 33

CHAPTER 2: THE LONE WOLF LIFESTYLE AND INTROVERSION REAWAKENED 35
   ARE ALL INTROVERTS LONE WOLVES? 36
   BEING A LONE WOLF 39

CHAPTER 3: THE PSYCHOLOGICAL EXPLORATION OF THE ALONE MIND 44
   THE NATURE OF THE ALONE MIND 47
   INTRINSICALLY MOTIVATED SOLITUDE 56

A POSITIVE EFFECT OF THE COVID-19 PANDEMIC 57

CHAPTER 4: HOW SOLITUDE COMPLIMENTS A HEALTHY SOCIAL LIFE 60

FIND THE BALANCE 63
YOU, YOUR SOCIAL CIRCLE, AND YOUR SOCIETY 68

CHAPTER 5: THE PERPETUAL DISTRACTION OF SOCIAL MEDIA 73

THE NEW CHAINS OF SOCIAL MEDIA 75
DESTRUCTION OF BODIES AND MINDS 77
DISCONNECT 82

CHAPTER 6: SILENT MEDITATION, SPIRITUAL SELF-DISCOVERY, AND THE SECRET TO SELF-ACTUALIZATION 85

KNOW THYSELF 88
SILENT MEDITATION 89
AWAKEN YOUR CREATIVITY 93
BEAUTY AND YOUR HOME 97
RECONNECT WITH NATURE 99
SPIRITUAL AWAKENING 104
SELF-ACTUALIZATION 110

CHAPTER 7: SKYROCKETING YOUR PRODUCTIVITY 112

LONE WOLVES AND SUCCESS 115
PROCRASTINATION, DISCIPLINE, FOCUS 118
Solving Procrastination 118
Being Disciplined 121
Becoming More Focused 122
MONK MODE 127

CHAPTER 8: THE SIX PILLARS OF SELF-SOVEREIGNTY IN A TRUE LONE WOLF 129

SELF-SOVEREIGNTY 131
First Pillar: Self-Discovery 132
Second Pillar: Self-Acceptance 133
Third Pillar: Self-Management 134
Fourth Pillar: Self-Growth 134

Fifth Pillar: Self-Confidence.. *135*
Sixth Pillar: Self-Reliance *137*
CONCLUSION **139**
A LAST DEFENSE OF SOLITUDE 140
REFERENCES **144**
IMAGE REFERENCES 154

Preface

Many struggle with loneliness. Something changes in their lives, and they find themselves in a new situation of isolation, not knowing how to cope with the overwhelmingly negative feelings that it brings them. Others struggle with the opposite. They enjoy being alone and want to spend more quality time in their own company, but they submit to the cultural pressure to be active participants in society or waste their precious alone time on unhealthy habits. Both cases suffer from a dearth of solitude, the positive state of spending time by yourself in an enjoyable, constructive, and productive manner. In the former, people don't know how to be alone, which makes them lonely. In the latter, people either don't get the solitude they need or, when they do, misuse it and turn it into loneliness. This book is dedicated to the introverts and the reclusive ones that don't know their hidden underlying power that sits within them, waiting to shine through once it is harnessed. Through an exciting and well-researched narrative, we explore the benefits of solitude, its place in our world, the obstacles we may face on our way to acquiring it, and how to use it. We takes the solitude-loving or needing reader on a spiritual journey of self-discovery and growth. Focusing on topics like self-development and personal responsibility, the book teaches us how to be authentic Lone Wolves, enabling us to become independent, sovereign individuals.

Introduction

Solitude is strength; to depend on the presence of the crowd is weakness. –Paul Brunton

The wolf pack stood at attention, listening to the blissful bleating of the sheep beyond the cover of the trees.

The drought and the recent forest fire had forced away many of the animals that would usually make up the majority of their meals, and the pack had to take the risk of attacking the flock of the nearby village. The wolves, their bellies hollowed out like an empty sack, took in the delicious aroma of the innocent and unsuspecting sheep. The beasts trembled with anticipation and hunger. But they had to wait because they felt the presence of the sheep dogs, as well as of the humans, who had gone inside their wooden homes with the coming of twilight.

Besides, none of these wolves was the leader. They were Betas, Deltas, and Omegas, and all knew their place in the wolf pack hierarchy. Some were more confident than others in the wisdom of their Alpha wolf, but there were those, even among the lowest of the low—the Omegas—who felt uncertain about this attack. Had the Alpha really thought this through? There was always a risk of one or two of their brothers or sisters falling dead during such attacks. This time the smell of the dogs—these slaves to humans, these traitors of the wolf's nature—was more intense than usual: The dogs were more than expected. And their masters, with their fire breathing weapons, had become more vigilant than ever. Had the Alpha wolf miscalculated? Were it not more prudent to move the pack somewhere else, to the other side of the mountain, where—if a wolf could trust the gossip of birds—there were hundreds of deer, hare, and pheasants.

But this didn't matter. The pack had to trust their leader and the elders. Wolves follow. That's their nature. Wherever the Alpha leads them, they will be beside him.

The big gray Alpha snorted. That was the signal. He sprang forth and disappeared through the trees; the rest of the pack followed. They could already taste the juicy meat between their jaws.

But the attack *was* a miscalculation. Although some of the wolves managed to bite a sheep leg or neck, none of them got to fill their bellies. The sheepdogs were a pack in their own right, and there were several humans guarding the flock. Two wolves were torn to pieces by the dogs, and seven fell dead to bullets. The Alpha accepted his failure and fled, followed by his pack. Enraged by their audacity, the humans and their dogs ran after them into the woods, determined to teach the beasts a lesson.

When the last human disappeared, a shadow emerged from the trees, a shadow that no one had noticed. It was the Loner, a Lone Wolf. He did not follow that pack, nor any other. But he had heard the ruckus and saw an opportunity. He threw himself over the fence that surrounded the flock. The sheep had nowhere to run. They were all his...

The Nature of Wolves and That of Humans

Wolves, like humans, are social animals. Most of them live in packs with a complex hierarchy, in which the majority obeys and follows, and a tiny minority leads. But even their leaders, when they fail or grow older, can be challenged, removed from authority, and be either killed or forced to accept a lower position in the dominance hierarchy.

Their societal system is rigid and highly ritualistic, and it allows for little, if any, freedom. Yet it has its benefits. When clustered together, wolves can hunt larger animals, and successfully attack human villages and flocks, thereby ensuring significant amounts of food. Moreover, it provides a safer environment for the raising of wolf pups, guaranteeing their security and healthy development and instructing them in the ways of the pack. Wolves also care for their elderly. Living in a group makes finding food easier for the older animals, and they are seldom left behind.

It is the same with humans. We are a social species, and our societal structures, hierarchies, and codes of behavior are among the most complex in nature. We live clustered together, be it in small villages, larger towns, or in megalopolises like New York City, London, Mumbai, or Shanghai. Human history itself begins with the self-preserving decision of our ancestors to stick together, to hunt, look after children, plow their lands, and build their cities and communities together. Just like with wolves, this brings us enormous benefits, ensuring the survival and continuation of our kind and the elaborate cultures and mythologies that we've developed.

Yet again, just like wolf packs, these benefits come at a cost. People who live in communities are required to behave in certain ways; to follow predetermined moral codes, religious beliefs, and political philosophies; to allow themselves to be molded by society; and to follow the trajectory of life that it dictates to them with obedience and even gratitude.

Although most people follow these demands without much or any quarrel, and although many of these demands can be regarded as truly beneficial to both the individual and the community, there are those among us—and among wolves—who prefer to go their own way. There are wolves who decide that they don't want to be just another obedient element in the pack. These Lone Wolves leave their community and choose to live by themselves, to be self-sufficient, to find their own path in life, and to learn how to not only survive, but also thrive in their solitude. Like them, humans "have biological needs for attachment, affiliation, and sociality, yet they continually seek to spend time in solitude" (Long & Averill, 2003, p. 22). This, more or less, applies to all of us. But some people need more solitude than others. They don't want to be members of the pack or society. They are the Lone Wolves.

You, Your Solitude, and This Book

If you're reading this book, it is likely that you're not a Beta wolf, following and serving the pack; nor an Alpha, who strives to be at the top of the dominance hierarchy by being strong and approved of by the community; nor a defenseless sheep that is fattened and used by those who're stronger than it; nor a dog, a charming slave to beings it regards as superior, even as gods.

No... You are a Lone Wolf, either of your own volition or because circumstances have forced you into a situation of social isolation.

If you are an already independent spirit, and live or are planning to live a more reclusive and individualistic lifestyle, and want to learn more about the necessary mindset for achieving it, the pages of this book will gift you the wisdom you seek.

Conversely, if you find yourself thrust into a position of loneliness that is challenging, or if you are tortured by a sense of aloneness, this book will help you to come to terms with your situation and show you how to turn it around and make it work for you. It will teach you how to enjoy your alone time and focus on productive and self-improving tasks, rather than waste your time thinking about what other people and the world are up to and trying to swallow the disgusting feeling of missing out on life.

The Lone Wolf's Way of Solitude is also for those who have low self-confidence and self-esteem, which makes it difficult for them to trust their own choices and judgment. It will teach you how to develop a sense of confidence, boost your productivity, and enable you to lead your life as an autonomous individual, who focuses their time and effort on their meaningful personal goals.

Suitable for all ages, this book explores the misconceptions and misunderstandings that surround the Lone Wolf's Way. It reveals the importance of solitude and the benefits it brings to an individual on their journey to independence and self-improvement. Avoiding total isolation and promoting balance, it shows you the importance of an appropriately solitary lifestyle, which results in an abundance of physical and mental health benefits that are required for achieving success in all areas of life. It will enable you to let go of dependencies that aren't necessary or are harmful, aid you in developing deeper focus, and unleash your individuality and potential.

Chapter by chapter, the book explains the differences between loneliness, aloneness, and solitude, and examines the importance of the last; it explores the differences between being introverted and being a Lone Wolf, and elaborates on the latter's potent lifestyle; it presents the psychology of those comfortable with solitude and argues that, contrary to popular opinion, living a solitary life actually improves your social interactions; it warns against the endless distractions around us, especially those of modern technology, and proposes strategies for coping with them; it lays down a path towards self-actualization and spiritual self-discovery; it focuses on ways of boosting your productivity and outlines the major pillars of the Lone Wolf's lifestyle.

My Own Journey

I've led a solitary life since I can remember, yet for a long time I refused to accept my reclusiveness, that way failing to see the many benefits that solitude had or could bring me. Like many, I never got adequate help or understanding from either family or friends, which thrust me into the consolation of social media, TV shows, YouTube, and gaming. Instead of using my alone time in productive and constructive ways, I wasted it in my blindness, unable to recognize the rich opportunities that my situation was serving me on a platter. Rather, I practiced so-called "preoccupied solitude," which is when you're alone and hating it, so you fill in the time that could be spent improving yourself with superficial entertainment and desperately try to 'connect' with people online, which, in most cases, is doomed to fail.

My life was approaching dystopian. While everyone around me seemed to know the proper way one was supposed to live and appeared to have a passion for something, a goal that they were pursuing, I was in a no man's land, lacking motivation to do anything and numbing my sadness with the hypnosis of the screen. Yet despite my refusal to accept true solitude and the inability to find self-love, I never sank into real depression. It was as if I'd always known, deep down, that my path would be different to that of most people and that I just needed more time to recognize and accept it. I saw what a precious gift life was, loved it, and wanted to honor it in my own way. Gradually, I accepted my solitude and, instead of wasting the time I had, I employed it, turning it into a resource that I used for self-improvement, learning new things and skills, reconnecting with nature, becoming fitter physically and mentally, and finding my purpose.

I wrote this book because I believe that this subject is not written or talked about enough, which leads to misconceptions about and prejudices against solitude and those who practice it. Understanding that, when done right, solitude is not simply beneficial, but a true blessing, can be helpful to all those who have always known that they're different and that society's ways are not for them. It can also aid those whose circumstances have suddenly changed and who find themselves living alone, in need of a way to adapt to that new state. It may also reveal the road to freedom for many who are slaves to toxic relationships with family members, false friends, or intimate partners. I want to see those who live in a secluded way similar to mine, or who want to give it a try, achieve through their own volition and willpower a greater understanding of what they can do with their valuable alone time.

Alone in Good Company

Although everyone has to tread on their own version of it, the Lone Wolf's path has been the choice of many great figures. Look up to them as an example of what you can achieve by yourself in your solitude. Many fictional characters who have captured our imagination and won our hearts are exceptional loners. Just think about Sherlock Holmes, Arya Stark, James Bond, Logan the Wolverine, Miss Marple, Bruce Wane aka Batman, and Albus Dumbledore.

If you want to be inspired by real people, just remember all the famous inventors, writers, artists, and scientists who were unashamed of their solitude. Albert Einstein, Isaac Newton, Elon Musk, Nikola Tesla, Emili Dickinson, Marcel Prous, Frida Kahlo, Karl Lagerfeld, Haruki Murakami, Virginia Woolf, and Franz Kafka are but the beginning of this illustrious list.

However, even if you're not a great artist, writer, or inventor, you can still have a fulfilling, productive, and spiritually-rich life as a Lone Wolf. In order to do that, you must understand that solitude is a tool. You can use it for good or let it morph into loneliness and do yourself evil with it. The Lone Wolf's Way chooses the good. It is a path that will lead to a life of truth, beauty, and goodness.

Chapter 1:

The Call for Solitude—The First Step of a Lone Wolf

Loneliness is the poverty of self; solitude is the richness of self. – Mary Sarton

His belly filled with juicy mutton, the Loner trotted through the woods, going further in, to the spot where he knew he would not be disturbed by anyone, except the birds and some moles and wood mice that were of no interest to him.

In a thicket of bracken, the wolf lay down and started cleaning his paws. He could hear the occasional muffled firing of the human weapons and a wolf howl or two, coming from the distance. The Loner remembered his wolf brothers and sisters. He hoped that they would be safe and that not too many would be killed by the villagers.

But they were to blame. The Loner had known for weeks that the humans were extra vigilant and that approaching the village would be folly. The pack were too mad to listen to the Alpha and his incompetent advisors. If they had rebelled against this absurd village raid and just moved to the other side of the mountain where there was more food, none of the wolves would be harmed. But what can one expect of wolves? They are followers and believe in authority. They can't stand to be alone.

Except for the Loner and a few others like him that he had heard about. However, he couldn't understand why there weren't more Lone Wolves like him. In his younger years, when he was still one of the pack, he could barely endure the constant presence of the others. They weren't nasty to him, but he often found their company overwhelming. And because he tended to seek solitude, often going on explorations or sleeping apart from them, they looked at him with little understanding and, frequently, with suspicion.

The Loner curled up on the ground covered in soft, cool moss, happy to be alone. If only his brothers and sisters could understand him, they would see...

Misconceptions About Solitude and the Lone Wolf Lifestyle

If you're a Lone Wolf full-time or at least have dipped your toes in the warm, soothing waters of solitude, you would have heard some, if not most, of these comments:

"What?! You don't want to go out?"

"But this is the best club in town! It'll be great!"

"Oh, come on! Everybody goes there!"

"Why are you like this?"

"You can't spend your whole life between four doors."

"Look, seeing people will do you good."

"Can't you just put in some effort and force yourself to go out?"

"You know what? Fine. Don't come. You can't interact with people anyway!"

"Frankly, I'm not surprised you don't want to see us anymore. You've always thought of yourself better than us."

"Why do you hate everyone? I mean... Do you hate me?!"

A Lone Wolf gets used to many of these comments. All of them come from people's sense of disbelief, pity, ridicule, anger, and even suspicion of the Lone Wolves' desire for solitude. This mustn't surprise you. After all, you're going against the grain; through your actions, you say "I don't need you, nor your company, ways, beliefs, or society." This is, in a way, a rejection, and rejection breeds resentment.

Still, although people's comments usually fall quite off the mark, some of them can be hurtful. This is why it is important to understand the misconceptions about solitude and the Lone Wolves' choices. Once you know where people's reactions come from, you will be able to address them in a more effective manner. That is... If you want to.

Solitude Is Total Self-Isolation

Many believe that Lone Wolves want total self-isolation, i.e., that they don't want any human company whatsoever, ever! It is true that there are people like this. Japan, for instance, is struggling with the *hikikomori* phenomenon, which involves thousands of young people, usually men, who isolate themselves and never come out, sometimes for years. However, most of these unfortunate young people have severe mental health issues that are causing their withdrawal from society.

Lone Wolves are not like this; they don't want to live in complete isolation, with zero social interactions. True, many solitary people find their alone time more fulfilling and exciting than the time they spend with others. But although they like their privacy and prefer to stay alone most of the time, this doesn't apply to every single minute of their existence. Yes, some do disapprove of society so much that they want nothing to do with it and go off to live like hermits, but these are extreme and rare cases. Most Lone Wolves are happy to socialize—for a while.

Being a Lone Wolf is about limits. They can't be around others for too long and need time alone to recharge their batteries before being ready for another social interaction or engagement. This is why they focus their attention on those around them who matter, i.e., their relatives, romantic partners, closest friends, and most valuable work partners or colleagues. This inevitably leads to their refusing many invitations and opportunities to meet new people.

Solitary People Never Want to Make Friends

Others suspect that people who prefer their alone time simply don't like to make new friends. As discussed above, choosing solitude is a form of rejection on both a personal and societal level, and many people—especially those who think very highly of themselves—may find this attitude offensive. But you can't be friends with everyone! Lone Wolves want and have friends, but not necessarily loads of them. They just want to focus on the few friends they already have and devote all their social time—which isn't much to begin with—to them. Their active interest in people has its limits, so they can't squander it. It doesn't mean that they're heartless and don't care for other people's feelings or company.

Moreover, sometimes it's exactly the opposite: Lone Wolves do want to make new friends, but they seek quality over quantity. Solitary people look on friendships as something precious, something to be grown and tended, like a rare and beautiful flower. Making new, *real* friends is a long and complicated process, and when Lone Wolves encounter people who're unwilling to put in the work and dedication required in that process, they can't see a reason to waste their own time on them. Really getting to know someone and learning to appreciate their good, as well as their bad, qualities takes time and effort, usually involving going through both good and bad experiences together.

Those who want quick and easy friendships and are quick to react negatively to Lone Wolves' initial lack of interest lose the opportunity to create a valuable and long-lasting relationship.

Solitary People Are Antisocial

There are those who maintain that people who prefer a more reclusive lifestyle are antisocial, in some cases going so far as to label them misanthropic. Some even believe that the 'negativity' of solitary people has killed all their desire to have fun.

This is not the case. Lone Wolves are confident individuals who like their own company and don't feel any particular need for that of others, even though they don't mind it on occasion. On the other hand, antisocial individuals are not necessarily happy in their own company, nor do they like that of others. In other words, many antisocial people find happiness or peace neither alone, nor in company. Being one of them must be a very difficult thing indeed.

Furthermore, the Lone Wolves love to have fun. But their idea of fun is very different from that of other people. They derive tons of enjoyment from their hobbies, projects, solitary trips, or simply reading great books. Lone Wolves' happiness doesn't depend on what others think or feel about them, nor on other people's company.

Solitary People Are Socially Inept

Some suspect that people who prefer to keep their distance from crowds do so simply because they don't know how to behave properly in the presence of others; that they haven't been properly socialized as children by their parents; or that they have some mental health issues that prevent them from interacting with people in a manner that is regarded as normal. Regrettably, there are many loners who are thus challenged, like the *hikikomori* people mentioned earlier, and others who live in loneliness, yet regard it as a state of torture.

This, however, is not the case for Lone Wolves, most of whom have the required social skills and manners to be with others and blend in with them. A Lone Wolf can have a beer with a few close buddies at a bar, or go to a black-tie cocktail party with their business partners and confidently participate in conversations with new people. They just choose to do so, not too often.

Solitary People Are Lazy

Many are of the opinion that people who are more reclusive are like this simply because they are indolent; that they are lazy and prefer to spend their days doing nothing; and that, to them, the very thought of going out and trying to socialize with new people requires an insurmountable amount of effort. Some would even go so far as to claim that solitary people live like parasites off their parents or partners, that they squander their inheritance, or work the bare minimum so they can survive, never putting in the effort that is required to build a career, create a family, finish a project, or do anything that is really worth doing.

Nothing could be further from the truth. The Lone Wolves are not lazy. They just prefer not to waste their valuable time and strength on relationships, acquaintances, and projects that they know would have little to no importance, that would yield nothing of worth. Most solitary people are hard-working, productive, entrepreneurial, and utterly dedicated to the things they believe in. Remember the list of successful solitary people from the 'Introduction'? Calling any of them lazy would be absurd.

Solitary People Have a Superiority Complex

And, of course, there are those who believe that Lone Wolves look on others from above, that they think they are some superior species who can look down upon the unenlightened and inauthentic commoners. In other words, people think they are pretentious and stuck up.

As it will be explored later in this book, it is true that Lone Wolves believe—and indeed, many of them are—privy to wisdom that others are either blind to or choose to ignore. However, if one feels superior to others, they would want to show this by always being on top. They would want to lead, to be the Alpha wolf, to win the gold medal, to get the award, to make the big bucks, to become the CEO of the company or the President of the country. Contrary to this, Lone Wolves have little to no craving for being regarded by other people or society as a whole as unique or distinguished. Humble and quiet, they are confident individuals who just want to be left alone to do their thing, whatever that may be.

These are the main prejudices against the practitioners of solitude. Naturally, such negative attitudes have harmful effects on them and on their image. As it happens, the prejudice against solitude is so prevalent that the very words "lone wolves" are often used to describe terrorists. Whenever there is a tragic shooting, be it at a school, on a street, or in a nightclub, journalists say that the perpetrator is "a Lone Wolf." No. They are not real Lone Wolves or at least not the kind that this book is about. These terrorists are mentally unstable, pathologically narcissistic, or utterly nihilistic. They are so unhappy or in love with themselves that they want to destroy the world, be it out of spite, hate, or pride. If they were people who were comfortable with their own company, they would not feel the need to turn against society and hurt it, usually killing dozens of innocents.

It would be great if people were more open about solitude and understood the real Lone Wolves. Yet, Lone Wolves ought to do their best not to act in ways that might appear too offensive and hermit-like to others. They need to learn how to communicate their preferences in a clear, polite manner, so that others will understand and respect—or at least humor—them. Knowing how to explain one's needs and desires prevents misunderstandings, and this is especially important with family members, close friends, and intimate partners.

Yet, in the end, the misunderstandings about the Lone Wolf's Way come from the inability of many to realize that the 'perfect' way to live is different for everybody. Some prefer company, others like solitude.

Loneliness and Aloneliness

The misconceptions outlined above come from a misunderstanding of terminology, namely not being able to see the differences between the states known as loneliness, aloneliness, and solitude.

Loneliness

Loneliness is a painful state of enforced detachment from society and unmet needs for human contact. It involves "a sense of abandonment or unwanted isolation" (Averill & Sundararajan, 2014, p. 91) and is often related to "psychological disorders, such as schizophrenia and depression" (Long & Averill, 2003, p. 22). Being lonely is a state, over which you have little to no control. It harms your mental health, which hinders you from acting upon your desire to put an end to your loneliness, thus perpetuating it. This enforced isolation is bad for everyone, but it can be especially detrimental for children and the elderly. When lonely, the former fail to develop crucial social skills that they will need later in life, while the latter becomes easier victims of Alzheimer's disease.

In many cases, the negative state of loneliness can be transformed into the positive state of solitude. This is easy for those who are cut out of Lone Wolves' cloth but have never tried to live in solitude and have suddenly found themselves in enforced isolation because of a divorce, death in the family, a pandemic, etc. Making the transition from loneliness to solitude would be relatively seamless for them. However, this transition will require hard work and strong character from those who are more extroverted and need the company of others.

Aloneliness

The negative feeling of loneliness emerges when you want and need solitude, but are denied it by circumstances that are out of your control. It is when you want to spend time by yourself but can't because stuff prevents you. A negative mirror image of loneliness, it is usually caused by too many and often overwhelming duties, such as work and family engagements.

Shy people often suffer from this, and, just like loneliness, loneliness can lead to depression and, in some cases, a mental breakdown. So, make sure to give yourself the solitude you want!

Solitude

The positive and often fruitful state of solitude is when you *choose* to spend time alone, away from others and the negative forces of the world. "[B]ased on the decision to be alone" (Averill & Sundararajan, 2014, p. 91), it is the "state of relative social disengagement, usually characterized by decreasing social inhibitions and increased freedom to choose one's mental and physical activities" (Long & Averill, 2003, p. 37). In other words, solitude is the often therapeutic quality of time you spend by yourself, during which you can focus on the things that you're really passionate about.

Some people need solitude more than others and are better able and happier to live apart from the pack, though not in total isolation from it. Even alone, they continue to be confident and content—or are that way exactly because they are alone. Solitary individuals are like everybody else in most things: They still have goals, dreams, and fears. However, they are more self-reliant and self-sufficient than others, usually mistrusting political and governmental authority and placing a high value on personal freedom. Those who love and pursue solitude are usually rational and more creative, and rarely strive for shallow status symbols, since they care little about how others perceive them.

An important thing to remember about solitude is that it is not the goal. For Lone Wolves, solitude is the means to achieve their goal, be it learning a new skill, inventing some new technology, writing a great novel or a collection of poems, painting a series of masterpieces, taking care of your garden and pets, contemplating the beauty and grandeur of nature, reading the books you want to read, meditating and finding inner peace.

Of course, solitude is not for everyone. Most Lone Wolves who pursue it are more or less introverted, i.e., wired for a more reclusive lifestyle. But developing a positive relationship with solitude is beneficial for everyone. For one thing, occupations such as art, writing, science, and research require long periods of being alone, and it's better to regard them as productive solitude, rather than tormenting loneliness. Moreover, at one point or another, everyone will find themselves in circumstances of isolation, and they had better be prepared for it. This is especially true for those with more fragile health and for elderly people.

The Benefits of Solitude for Extroverts

It may sound odd to say it, but solitude can be of enormous benefit to very extroverted people. Extroverts are those who are always out and about, who love the company of others, and who seem actively engaged in many group activities.

They crave other people's society; it is like a high to them. However, they often push themselves too far, reaching their limit and failing to read the signs that their body and mind send them, informing them that it's time to chill out and retreat for a moment. An extroverted lifestyle is active and often leads to burnout.

In most cases, it doesn't even occur to extroverts that solitude may be a good way for them to relax and recharge. That is why when they step over the border of their limit, they realize they absolutely need to be alone for a time and retreat in a violent manner, often creating dramatic scenes.

To avoid such extremes, they can simply spend some time alone. But solitude can help extroverts in other ways, too. It can be argued that at the core of every Lone Wolf there is someone who likes their own company, while at the core of every extrovert, who always wants to be surrounded by others, is someone who either dislikes themselves or is scared of confronting their nature and character. Extroverts are often riddled with insecurities. They are afraid that they may be insufficient, unattractive, irrelevant, and unworthy of the attention of the people, whose presence they constantly seek.

Such insecurities make them disconnected from and even hateful of themselves. Whenever they are left alone, they are not in a state of solitude, but one of loneliness that is difficult to endure. Getting used to solitude is good for extroverts because it makes them confront their true selves. When they do it, they will either like it or not. If the latter, they will see where they need to improve and work towards it. In other words, the thing that they try to avoid most of all turns out to be the key to their mental wellbeing.

Solitude as Rebellion

One of the protective mechanisms that societies use to ensure their survival is the institutionalization of most aspects of human behavior and making them work for their own benefit and continuation, rather than to their detriment. This is the case with solitary people, albeit only to a limited degree. Both Western and Eastern societies have institutionalized solitude in the form of monasticism. It has brought them many benefits, such as remarkable scholarly achievements and the perpetuation of "cultural traditions through examples of sacrifice and spiritual devotion" (Long & Averill, 2003, p. 39). Moreover, monasticism ensures a role for some individuals who would not be regarded as fitting for 'normal' society.

Yet, monasticism is an exception, and a tiny one at that. For the most part, deciding to leave society and lead a more secluded existence is regarded as an act of rebellion against that same society, its political systems, and the moral principles of its people. The norm in every major culture is to stick with your community, and when you try to go against this, even partially, you become a dangerous rebel, because your actions say: "I disapprove of you and I don't need you." And if too many people from a particular society dare do this, it will be their end.

That said, "solitude has played a vital role in the history of societies" (Long & Averill, 2003, p. 37). Most of the greatest artistic and scientific geniuses were people who valued their alone time, as were many philosophers, political leaders, and—most consequently—figures like Jesus, Muhammad, and Buddha, who founded potent religious movements. Good artists know that, if they want to see mistakes in their painting, they should stand back and look at the canvas from a distance. Perhaps it's the same with societies: People who like solitude are able to look at them from the outside and see aspects that can be changed, be it for the better or worse.

But rebelling against societal demands through solitude is mostly beneficial to those who are daring enough to attempt it: The Lone Wolves. Sociocultural standards always try to force you on a path that may not be yours. If you don't resonate with your culture's idea of who you ought to be, you will be seeking a way out. Solitude is one such way, since it "reduces the need for impression management without imposing a pattern of behavior to which one feels pressured to conform" (Long & Averill, 2003, p. 37). This is empowering because it is freedom.

Chapter 2:

The Lone Wolf Lifestyle and Introversion Reawakened

A man can be himself only so long as he is alone, and if he does not love solitude, he will not love freedom, for it is only when he is alone that he is really free. –Arthur Schopenhauer

The wolf opened his eyes.

There was no one. It was quiet. Or as quiet as the forest could be. The sky beyond the branches was the color of ripening wild strawberries: The sun was about to rise.

As was the Loner. He yawned, rose to his feet, took his time stretching every muscle in his strong body, and then shook the remnants of sleep from his fur.

The wolf started his journey. He had decided that he should move to the other side of the mountain. He had lived there for a while and knew that the climate beyond the peaks was better than the one here. The storm clouds gathered there and watered the slopes and woods, and there was plenty of food and shelter for everyone.

The journey would be neither short nor safe. Yet he knew a secret path that would lead him there. No one used it, because no one knew it. And no one knew it, for he was the one who made it.

As he climbed up among the tall, gnarled trees, he thought about the wolf pack from last night. It used to be his pack. He still remembered most of the wolves in it. He liked some of them, though many he could not stand. And there were those who were very much like him: They disliked being in a pack, disliked following, obeying. Still, they kept quiet, they kept following, not having the guts to walk away and make their own paths.

Unlike him—he did it and did not regret it. The Loner walked on in solitude, and that empowered him and made him feel like independence itself...

Are All Introverts Lone Wolves?

Introversion is always compared to extroversion, but it is seldom compared to the way of the Lone Wolf. Are they different? Are all introverted, solitude-loving, independence-seeking, self-sufficient individuals? Or are the Lone Wolf's preferences and lifestyle those of some introverted people, but not all?

The distinction between introverts and extroverts started with the work of Carl Jung at the beginning of the last century. Later, psychologists developed the Big Five Personality Traits theory, which is a convenient taxonomy of some human personality traits. One of the Big Five is extroversion. People who score high on the extroversion trait are more likely to prefer busy environments, to seek crowds and social interactions, to act in an impulsive manner, and to avoid being on their own.

Introverts are those who score low in extroversion. Most of them prefer to spend their time alone in calmer settings and may appear more reserved. Introverted people "meet their stimulation needs much more easily and can become overstimulated in highly social contexts, thus preferring quieter activities" (Zelenski et al., 2014, p. 184). This condition, as with most personality traits, can be caused by the genetic inheritance one gets from their biological parents; by environmental influences, usually in early childhood, that are caused by the way parents, teachers, peers, and others interact with one; or by the two of these combined.

This dependency on a rich variety of shaping factors means that there are many types of introverts. Some crave total isolation from others and the world, while most are happy with smaller companies or the occasional interaction with a number of close relations and friends. Some hate the time they spend by themselves, while others love solitude and regard it as a time for meditation that they can use to explore their own thoughts. Most of them find socializing draining, and although it's not necessary for introverts to have social anxiety, many of them do. Not a few of them are inhibited, in the sense that they are more restrained in their words and actions and therefore need more time to consider what to say or do. Most introverts are very self-conscious—often to a fault—and don't do well in situations of conflict or debate.

This makes it clear that most introverts are not necessarily Lone Wolves. They may well want the company of others, but find it too much to handle and don't know how to operate in a social setting; or they may be happy with their loneliness, but still lack the confidence and purpose that every true Lone Wolf has.

However, although some extroverts can be Lone Wolves—or at least learn to appreciate and treasure periods of solitude—most Lone Wolves are introverts. The Lone Wolf Way is a deep and powerful form of introversion. Like all introverts, they prefer solitude, but this doesn't mean that they have social anxiety or that they can't interact with others. Lone Wolves aren't shy, and, whenever it's necessary, they can defend themselves and their beliefs with confidence.

And they have to, for people often look upon them with a disapproving eye that fails to see how glorious it is to be a Lone Wolf.

Being a Lone Wolf

At some point in their lives, all people are given the choice to walk the path of the Lone Wolf. This happens when they're thrust into loneliness or seclusion by unforeseen or unavoidable circumstances, such as a personal or societal tragedy or the discovery of a piece of information that makes them look upon the world in a different way. Such a change in their situation enables them to realize that they're no longer in their old, familiar world; that, like the hero in an epic story, there is an odyssey of discovery and self-realization before them; and that they are given the choice to take a new path.

When some find themselves in such a place of intense loneliness, they may decide to try to embrace it and make it work for them, instead of falling into depression and attempting to rejoin society, even though it didn't make them that happy in the first place. It is a brave thing to do, because it declares: "I've made the decision to be on my own and to think on my own." Some people in that novel situation may see the faults of their previous existence and, although they miss some of its comforts and security, decide to do their best to live in solitude. And there are those who, whenever their circumstances change in a drastic manner, realize that the Lone Wolf's path is perfect for them; that it is as if they have been created to go on this exciting, constructive, and productive individualistic journey.

For the Lone Wolf is someone who is an individualist. They are the person who decides to take the lonely and idiosyncratic path, who leaves much or all of their old life behind and often—though not always—decides not to do the things or become the person others expect them to. They become different and stand apart from the community. Freedom and truth stand high in their hierarchy of virtue. Lone Wolves trust their inner voice and try—and hopefully fulfill—their spiritual destinies.

This is quite a lot. No wonder many who can or should try this way of living are afraid to do it. Taking the first step *is* terrifying. Taking many steps after the first one is equally frightening. Deciding to be individualistic and a Lone Wolf means that they will probably be rejected by society or, at least, by parts of it. Condemnation is to be expected, even from those closest to you, and being branded as 'other,' 'weird,' and even 'suspicious' is almost inevitable. Friends, loved ones, and relatives may turn their backs on you, even if you don't want to isolate yourself from them completely. The act of deciding to take the independence of solitude that is the fertile ground of individuality is so revolutionary, that it may even go against our biological predisposition to be accepted as part of the whole.

On the other hand, there are the potential Lone Wolves who are reluctant to embrace this way of life, because it will cast them into uncharted territory. When you're a Lone Wolf, you are on your own in *terra incognita*. You will have to be the one to find the rules of the game. There will be little to no instruction. You will have to cut your own path through the thicket of the dark forest, hoping that you're going in the right direction.

Making mistakes is inevitable. You will fail once, twice, many times, and maybe you will have to start again.

In other words, when you are a Lone Wolf, responsibility lies with you. You have to do all the work, to be self-sufficient and self-reliant. You're the knight who is the hero of your story, but you're also the blacksmith who forges the hero's armor and sword. The responsibility is so great that even if you want to go on that journey, you may not know where to start.

Well... these pages are one such start.

The start of the Lone Wolf's journey, which is one of discovery. On it, you have the chance to realize your true destiny. The Lone Wolf's path is not one of mundane, humdrum boredom; it is your own soul path. On it, you may grow on multiple levels: You will become spiritually-awakened and more emotionally mature; your creativity and productivity will be unleashed; you will see new opportunities and discover the people who really care for you, those who accept you and support your choices; you will be more excited about the world and see life as a thrilling adventure; and you will gain new levels of self-understanding and respect.

Of course, the lifestyle of one Lone Wolf will be very different from that of another. That's the point! Lone Wolves are individualists who make their own rules and their own way. Still, there are commonalities between them. Be they rich or of modest means, men or women, younger or older, solitary people want to be left to their own devices. They value their independence and live a life that is focused on what is important to them.

Able to get things done, Lone Wolves are quiet and observant. Since creativity requires dedication and work in seclusion for days on end, for months even, many solitary people are creative, be it in the realm of art, literature, music, thought, or science. Filled with mysterious motivation, they hate wasting time on distractions and try to avoid them. They do not need society to stimulate them, they are good at controlling themselves and are filled with self-understanding and self-compassion.

For them, privacy is of crucial importance. The company of most others is beyond boring for them, and they don't seek people's approval. They nurture only their few and most precious relationships with people who value their friendship, love, and deep loyalty. This is achievable, because Lone Wolves find balance in life; the golden middle between spending some time with family and friends and the time they share only with themselves.

Making mistakes is inevitable. You will fail once, twice, many times, and maybe you will have to start again.

In other words, when you are a Lone Wolf, responsibility lies with you. You have to do all the work, to be self-sufficient and self-reliant. You're the knight who is the hero of your story, but you're also the blacksmith who forges the hero's armor and sword. The responsibility is so great that even if you want to go on that journey, you may not know where to start.

Well… these pages are one such start.

The start of the Lone Wolf's journey, which is one of discovery. On it, you have the chance to realize your true destiny. The Lone Wolf's path is not one of mundane, humdrum boredom; it is your own soul path. On it, you may grow on multiple levels: You will become spiritually-awakened and more emotionally mature; your creativity and productivity will be unleashed; you will see new opportunities and discover the people who really care for you, those who accept you and support your choices; you will be more excited about the world and see life as a thrilling adventure; and you will gain new levels of self-understanding and respect.

Of course, the lifestyle of one Lone Wolf will be very different from that of another. That's the point! Lone Wolves are individualists who make their own rules and their own way. Still, there are commonalities between them. Be they rich or of modest means, men or women, younger or older, solitary people want to be left to their own devices. They value their independence and live a life that is focused on what is important to them.

Able to get things done, Lone Wolves are quiet and observant. Since creativity requires dedication and work in seclusion for days on end, for months even, many solitary people are creative, be it in the realm of art, literature, music, thought, or science. Filled with mysterious motivation, they hate wasting time on distractions and try to avoid them. They do not need society to stimulate them, they are good at controlling themselves and are filled with self-understanding and self-compassion.

For them, privacy is of crucial importance. The company of most others is beyond boring for them, and they don't seek people's approval. They nurture only their few and most precious relationships with people who value their friendship, love, and deep loyalty. This is achievable, because Lone Wolves find balance in life; the golden middle between spending some time with family and friends and the time they share only with themselves.

This time—their solitude—is the source of their strength. They know better than anyone else that the habit of spending time alone should be treated as an essential act of self-love, just like having a good diet and exercising regularly.

That solitude transforms them into spirits who can achieve total liberation from society's chains and, indeed, from the chains forged by the bad aspects of their own character. They're on the path to liberation from both external and internal bondage. Unable to tolerate nonsense and untruths, they have a strong moral compass and bravely face challenges.

Maybe the greatest test that they have to pass is facing themselves. Lone Wolves have a vast inner world and a rich inner life that makes socializing largely unnecessary. They have to learn how to deal with their emotions and how to manage themselves. Lone Wolves have to, and are often more than willing to, face certain truths about themselves, society, and the world that most people refuse to accept or even think about. Their solitary life helps them accept their own existence and clarifies their high goals.

Be a Lone Wolf. Find out what you want. Love yourself. But you know what you love. Deep self-understanding is compulsory. Know your nature. Don't worry if you're afraid. It's to be expected. Listen to your instincts. Know your mind. The Lone Wolf's Way is an inward journey, an exploration of the cosmos inside you that is a reflection of the cosmos around you.

Chapter 3:

The Psychological Exploration of the Alone Mind

I restore myself when I'm alone. –Marilyn Monroe

Yes. The path was exactly where he remembered it: Behind the stone that looks like a bear's claw, with a thicket of blackthorn on its left that reeks of dead badger.

The sun was up in the sky, though there was still time till the great heat of the day. Here the wood was beginning to thin and he could feel the wind blowing between the trunks of the tall pine trees and see snippets of sky above him, with small clouds chasing each other through the bright blue of the sky.

The Loner took the path and started a calm and slow climb. He almost showed his teeth in a smile. He loved walking in these secluded parts of the mountain. Meeting anyone here was unlikely, apart from the occasional mountain goat, who would look at him from a distance with suspicion, or an aloof eagle, who were so proud that they didn't even pay attention to wolves. The Loner understood them well. They also liked their solitude, and he was grateful to them for not encroaching on his alone time.

To him, walking these paths was like walking in his own mind. It was sharp and rocky, but clean, with the occasional soft and fragrant corners of moss and blooming thyme; it was open to the sky and let in the sun, moon, and stars; it allowed for clear and measured thought, for adamant Lone Wolf logic, and gave him space for going over the vivid images and smells of his past, as well as those he wanted to or feared he might encounter in the future.

But there were dark corners in his mind too. Narrow crevices in the stone, hollows, and caves that were filled with blackness, bones, slime, and, in some cases, even cold water of treacherous depths. These places were scary, even to the Loner. But he knew them well. He had confronted them long ago in his isolation. He was brave enough to push aside his fears and to step inside the darkness of his mind, he had seen what it contained. The wolf had confronted the ancient beasts, all teeth, claws, guilt, fears, shame, and evil, and he had defeated them. Some of them he killed, pulling them to the surface of the earth where he could see them better in the sunlight and realize that they were not that scary after all. Others he wounded and sealed deep inside his mind-caves with big boulders, so that they could never crawl out and pester him.

Yes. The Loner's mind was a vast network of paths, tunnels, and caves, but he knew them well and could walk them with as much confidence as he walked up that rocky mountain...

The Nature of the Alone Mind

Most research suggests that there is "robust evidence that people scoring higher on extraversion report higher levels of happiness" (Zelenski et al., 2014, p. 187) than introverts. That said, the legitimacy of the strong association between happiness and extraversion "depends somewhat on how happiness and extraversion are defined" (Zelenski et al., 2014, p. 195).

The concept of happiness is something quite unclear and, regrettably, elusive. First, everyone knows that happiness is subjective. One woman would feel content at home, surrounded by her children and husband; another would be happiest when she solves important problems for the business, to which she had decided to devote most of her time; a third wants nothing more than to sit quietly and write a book. In other words, being happy depends on your definition of happiness.

Furthermore, happiness is not a permanent state one can achieve. It is, at best, a fleeting moment and, at worst, an illusion. One explanation for why most introverts score lower on happiness during scientific research is that they don't fool themselves. Extroverts fill their time with interactions with others, many of them meaningless, often with the objective of filling in the silence that they would experience were they by themselves. It is this silence that fear, for it forces them to look at the world without their rose-colored glasses and—even worse for some—makes them confront themselves and all the uncomfortable truths about their past, present, and future eventualities, about their choices, character, and fears.

Unlike them, most introverts are more than capable of facing their inner worlds and looking at the world and human nature with honesty, understanding, and acceptance. Introverts don't fool themselves into thinking that the world is something that it isn't, and they have no need for unnecessary communal activities that would numb the fears and desperation most extroverts feel when left alone with their thoughts.

Moreover, research has shown that, when pressed, introverts can act in an extroverted manner for a time, which affects them in positive ways, while extroverts are usually unable to draw any positives from acting as introverts. In other words, evidence to date suggests that "introverts appear to more easily regulate their behavior [while] extraverts suffer cognitive and emotional deficits when asked to act introverted" (Zelenski et al., 2014, p. 196). Contrary to expectations, introverts are better able to adapt to different circumstances than extroverts, probably because introverts are more attuned to themselves and the world.

That said, it is likely "that prolonged periods of extraverted behavior would drain introverts" (Zelenski et al., 2014, p. 196) and have palpable negative consequences for them. It is, therefore, desirable for them to seek and achieve solitude.

One possible reason for introverts to want and need to live in relative seclusion is that they score higher on the Sensory Processing Sensitivity (SPS) chart. This is a personality trait that indicates a person's ability to process both external and internal stimuli, such as physical sensations, interactions with others, information, thoughts, and emotions. Some people are able to cope with huge loads of sensory stimuli, while others have their limits. The former, perhaps, overlook many details and don't examine much of the received information, thus coping with it. On the other hand, the latter see and explore the many details presented to them, get overwhelmed, and, therefore, need to retreat from the world into a place of solitude to manage this data overload.

There are many among us like this; about 20% of people have high SPS and the percentage among children is even higher. These people are very sensitive, but not by choice and not necessarily in a bad way. True, having high SPS may lead to anxiety and the many physical and mental problems that come with it. However, if the person knows what they need to know to avoid or manage the sensory overload and gets it, then they will thrive. "Biology has provided a need or preference for solitude, and some of us need or prefer more solitude than... others" (Long & Averill, 2003, pp. 38–39). These people are introverts, and solitude for them is a necessity. Most Lone Wolves are among them, and solitude for them is the compulsory state that maintains their sanity and gives them the energy to cope with, indeed, thrive in the world.

That said, solitude is not a state frozen in time. It is something fluid, something that changes into other things. Even for the most independent of Lone Wolves, solitude can sometimes turn to loneliness. Although loneliness is a negative and painful state that we should better avoid, it "may also be a source of benefit" that motivates "individuals to seek solutions to problems that might otherwise be allowed to fester" (Averill & Sundararajan, 2014, p. 101). In other words, it points the mind of the Lone Wolf to things that need sorting, and gives them time to examine them and the opportunity to fix them. It is important to remember that moments of loneliness are unavoidable and, actually, completely natural. If a person in isolation—be it voluntary or forced—never goes through periods of loneliness, "we might suspect something is amiss, for loneliness… Is part of our human heritage" (Averill & Sundararajan, 2014, p. 101); it may be the sign of some serious form of psychopathy.

There are many ways that Lone Wolves can chase away the occasional episodes of loneliness. Recreation and diversion are among them. Usually, doing what you love, what is enjoyable and feels rewarding, usually pays off and transforms the lonely place into one of comfortable and productive solitude. Diverting oneself can be similar, but it depends on what you do as a diversion. If you plunged into a rich and complex book that is exciting and intellectually and mentally challenging, then this would likely have a positive effect. If you glued your eyes to your phone screen and used every second at your disposal to watch new bizarre YouTube videos, Instagram reels, or porn clips, then you would probably do yourself more harm than good, as will be explored in a later chapter.

One of the main characteristics of true Lone Wolves is that, by experiencing solitude, they "are attuned to dialogue with their own mind or conscience" (Gordon, 2022, p. 1). This is a rare emotional refinement and maturity that is either encoded in Lone Wolves' software or is within their grasp, and they only have to make the small effort to reach out and take it. It enables them to tackle moments of loneliness by equipping them with an important tool, which is nostalgia. This romantic state "contains elements of longing, reminiscence, and intimacy" and "involves the psychological work of emotional transformation" (Averill & Sundararajan, 2014, p. 102). It is the skill of looking back on your past, examining your present, and projecting yourself into the future in a wise, realistic manner that is colored by feelings of understanding, acceptance, and stoicism, and enables you to see the good, the beautiful, and the true in the world around you and your experiences, as well as to recognize patterns of meaning in your life. This skill is the result of life experience, learning, and of spending time in solitude. For solitude is the shelter, where we find the mental freedom, we need to develop moral courage, clarity, and creativity, as well as the ability to problem-solve.

Another way of calling this mature and productive mental state is "designer environment." For solitude to be effective, and not to turn to loneliness or pseudo-solitude—in which the alone person wastes their time with distractions—it has to happen in a designed environment. Almost all animals create their own habitats of physical and social safety, but we humans can create such a habitat in our cognitive space. Designer environments are "ideal mental worlds" (Averill & Sundararajan, 2014, p. 100). However, they're not 'ideal' in an unrealistic and self-delusional kind of way; they are ideal, because they are effective. Our designer environment is the inner cathedral of our mind, which we have partially built ourselves consciously and partially discovered during explorations in our subconscious. It is a space that we know and are able to manage, and through that, we're able to manage ourselves, for the cathedral of our mind is actually us.

True solitude is the result of a subtle balance between isolation from most of society, communion with a few chosen people and with yourself, independence and self-sufficiency, and deep self-knowledge. Many people desire solitude, but to achieve authentic solitude, you need to have a beautiful mind. And beautiful minds can be achieved through solitude. The mental journey of a Lone Wolf is an ouroboros; a serpent that eats its own tail, an endless cycle of self-discovery that leads to ultimate enlightenment.

However, to achieve authentic solitude and to use it well, it is best for a person to have acquired certain capabilities, many of them age-related. The most important of them are "(a) the successful negotiation of attachment processes in infancy, (b) the development of advanced reasoning skills, and (c) the development of the propensity for reflexive thought, as influenced by previous social interactions" (Long & Averill, 2003, pp. 37–38). Individuals who are thus developed, are more balanced and fortified against most challenges that may come from without and from within.

And being thus balanced and fortified is important for Lone Wolves, because solitude provides opportunities "for loosening and subsequent reconstruction of cognitive structures" (Long & Averill, 2003, p. 39). When we don't interact with others, we are more able to create new cognitive worlds and to transition between them. This can literally transform our brain structure and, therefore, the way we think. When this happens for the worse, then the solitude one was experiencing turns out to have been pseudo-solitude, i.e., loneliness. When the change is for the better, then it is authentic solitude. Yet such changes are profound and frightening things. It's no wonder why many prefer to avoid them, and in the case of the unprepared, it is the wiser course of action. "[I]n order to benefit from solitude, the individual must be able to draw on inner resources to find meaning in a situation in which external supports are lacking" (Long & Averill, 2003, p. 40).

While this ability is determined largely by personality characteristics and early development—both almost or entirely out of our control—it is also determined by the immediate environment, in which solitude is happening, and by the individual's ability to be alone with their own thoughts. If the environment is one of comfort and safety, and if the individual has the option of reconnecting to society if they so choose, then the isolation can easily be transformed into solitude. Similarly, if the individual has a balanced mental life, i.e., no serious past traumas that torment them or, if they have gone through traumas, they have managed to address and come to terms with them, then they will be able to stay alone with their memories and thoughts. Furthermore, the beliefs that an individual has about themselves and the world are also of crucial importance. If they harbor some dark, hopelessly nihilistic views about human nature, themselves, and the whole universe, then they had better distract themselves with the company of others and some light entertainment. If, on the other hand, they follow a nuanced and profound philosophical or religious system, then they have a better chance to make solitude work for them. Lastly, their previous experience with solitude may also be decisive. "[I]f the person's solitude-related beliefs and memories result in anxiety with respect to lack of volition or to social disconnection, then she or he will likely retreat into loneliness" (Long & Averill, 2003, p. 40). But if they don't have any preconceived notions about isolation or have good memories of solitude, then they will be able to thrive in it.

While people can't decide aspects of their psychology nor determine their early development, most of us can influence our beliefs and moral systems, as well as work and better our character. Doing this is important, because solitude is crucial to self-growth. In solitude, the individual confronts their choices, actions, and results and has to judge them. In solitude, you become your own judge, and you will be the harshest but most accurate of all judges. This process of self-examination is the path to self-growth and self-actualization.

Intrinsically Motivated Solitude

We can wait for isolation to come to us, believing that we will easily transform it into solitude. And make no mistake, isolation is coming. Be it because of separation, rejection, death, illness, old age, or government decree during a pandemic or other turbulent times, you will find yourself in a situation where your only companion will be the one inside your head. It is better, therefore, not to wait and see what will happen when this time comes, but to prepare for it by practicing intrinsically motivated solitude, which is the best way to experience the positive effects of solitude.

Loneliness is often a state we cannot change. It "generates an inertia of its own, as lonely people tend to increase their own feelings of loneliness" (Amichai-Hamburger & Schneider, 2014, p. 317). Intrinsically motivated solitude is something we design. It is a pristine edifice of our own making, into which we retreat for a time of self-discovery, self-development, and to work on anything that is important to us. It is something we control, and we can always rejoin society if we want to. It is a solitude that can be total and prolonged, or partial and short, even momentary, as when we read a book or take a walk in a park by ourselves. It is a conscious and luxurious withdrawal, allowed by the awareness that being by yourself is not staring at the abyss, but a glorious genesis, a new beginning of potential and creation.

A Positive Effect of the COVID-19 Pandemic

The COVID-19 pandemic and the global reaction to it were calamities, the proportions of which humanity had never seen. Hundreds of millions contracted the virus, millions died, and the magnitude of the economic repercussions of lockdowns is yet to be seen on its full and frightful scale.

Moreover, an unknown number of people suffered and still suffer from mental health problems caused by the pandemic and the general bleak atmosphere and circumstances of 2020 and 2021. One of the main causes of this second, largely unnoticed pandemic, was the series of lockdowns that were imposed with different lengths and severity in different parts of the world. "Social isolation associated with quarantine can be the catalyst for many mental health sequelae, even in people who were previously well" (Usher et al., 2020, p. 2). Among the issues that may be caused by lockdowns are insomnia, acute stress and mood disorders, anxiety, and depression. Moreover, "[t]he negative mental health impacts do not simply stop but continue following the quarantine period" (Usher et al., 2020, p. 2), resulting in conditions like posttraumatic stress disorder (PTSD) and avoidance behavior. All are vulnerable to the negative effects of lockdowns, but this is especially true of those who are already in a vulnerable group, like children, the elderly, and people with health issues.

Finding a silver-lining to the whole pandemic tragedy is quite difficult. And yet… And yet! This global loss of the freedom to go out and socialize with people outside of our households has helped many of us realize our fragility and relatedness. It opened our eyes to the many challenges of loneliness and the vital importance of solitude. Among other things, during lockdowns, people suffered either from the lack of solitude or from excessive amounts of loneliness. The former tormented people, who were locked inside with their families and had to be with them 24/7 for weeks, even months on end. No matter how much you love someone, be they your parent, partner, or child, you cannot be with them all the time. This lack of time spent alone is exhausting and quickly becomes a source of stress. The latter plagued those who lived alone, those who either had no one in their lives or whose friends and family lived far away, and those whom the pandemic starved of face-to-face human interaction and physical touch.

In the first case, people who had regular doses of solitude, maybe even without realizing it, found themselves overwhelmed by the constant presence of others. In the second, people who were not accustomed to solitude, or at least not to one of these proportions, craved human society. The pandemic forced everyone to acknowledge their vulnerabilities and to realize that quality time spent alone is one of the ways to overcome them. Practicing intrinsically motivated solitude helped people improve mentally, or at least remain stable, during the pandemic. Of course, as was explored above, the ability to cultivate solitude depends on many personal qualities and environmental circumstances—such as having some financial security and the necessity to be quarantined in a safe space. If, during a lockdown, one is trapped in an apartment with an abuser, be they a parent or a partner, finding solitude would be next to impossible, unless one is of a really stoic and strong disposition and is able to retreat into their own consciousness.

Thankfully, most people don't have to live in such harrowing conditions, even during lockdowns, which enables them to reconnect with themselves and find authentic solitude. After the initial shock of the first two or three weeks of lockdown, people realized that they needed to take better care of themselves in ways that involved spending time alone. They started new or restarted old hobbies, found time to read their favorite old or exciting new books, decided to develop new skills or complete a new project, started working out more, and reconnected with nature on walks and bike rides in parks and woods. This made them feel the importance of achieving the right balance between spending time alone and with others; it made them more mature individuals and more valuable members of society.

Chapter 4:

How Solitude Compliments a Healthy Social Life

In order to understand the world, one has to turn away from it on occasion; in order to serve men better, one has to hold them at a distance for a time. –Albert Camus

Up and up, he climbed. Soon the pine trees were left behind him, and he continued to walk among twisted juniper bushes and rocks covered in grayish lichen.

The Loner was a bit tired from the climb, but he preferred to rest after he reached the mountain ridge. To him, rest was sweetest after he'd made the journey or finished a hunt. Besides, the ridge wasn't that far. Soon he would get to the widening of the path that was like a balcony of rocks looking over the forests below, and the walk to the top of it would take him no more than a couple of hours. At the top, he would rest, maybe even find a nook or a crack with rainwater to quench his thirst…

The wolf stopped in his tracks.

He didn't move a muscle; he simply fixed his yellowish gaze on something before him that he could not see because the path curved behind a wall of rocks. He could not see it, yet he could smell it. The smell of another wolf. Its distinct notes were flying towards him on the soft breeze, which meant that the wolf that could not see him couldn't smell him either. That was good, that was safer.

The Loner breathed in deeply. No. The smell was not that of *a* wolf, but of *two* wolves. Two beasts of his kind were waiting on the path widening ahead of him. The Loner hadn't smelled their tracks, but there were other paths that led to that widening, and maybe they had reached it via one of them.

What was he to do? He could turn back and find another path, though this may take days. Or he could just stay here and wait and see if the wolves would walk off without noticing him or if they'd make a turn towards him and find him. He liked neither of these options. The first would prolong his journey to the other side of the mountain, while the latter made him passive, as if he was waiting for something to happen to him, not having his life under his control. No, that won't do.

The third option was to step forward and confront them. That was a risk, but he took it.

The Loner took the turn and stepped on the widening of the path, startling the two big wolves that were resting there. They jumped to their feet, the hair on their backs bristling, and fixed their eyes on him; one of them growled quietly. The Loner didn't tremble, for now he recognized one of the two. The older wolf in front of him was from his old pack. He was the best scout wolf that the Loner knew. The other wolf was much younger and was probably a scout-in-training.

Time passed. The growl of the young one soon died out. They didn't attack the Loner. That was good: He won't have to attack them either. This meant that he could simply walk by and continue on his way. But there was no rush. He had not been face to face with another wolf for very long. Since they weren't aggressive, it wouldn't hurt him to spend some time with them. It could even be pleasant.

He took the first step. The Loner sniffed the older wolf. When the youth saw that they knew each other, he greeted the Loner and made his acquaintance.

It turned out that, after the problems with the villagers from last night, their Alpha had finally decided to lead his pack to the other side of the mountain and had sent these two scouts to find an easier way over the ridge. They had found the path, but soon it would branch out into several directions, all of which—except one—were dead ends.

The Loner decided to take the two of them with him. He would show them the proper way and then, once they knew it, they would go back and tell their pack, while he would continue onwards. Yes, that was his path, but he didn't mind sharing it with others. Nor did he mind their company. For a time…

Find the Balance

Solitude "can be defined as the absence of human activity" (Gordon, 2022, p. 1); it is also the chief component of privacy, setting us free from the bondage of society and enabling us to focus on ourselves and our goals. However, "[s]olitude may occur at the edges of society, but it has meaning only within a social context" (Long & Averill, 2003, p. 37).

As said before, being a hermit is not for everyone. The percentage of people who can live in absolute isolation is minuscule. Most of us will forever be chained to other individuals and to our society and its culture, mainly through relationships and the responsibilities that come with them. And this is not entirely bad. Some of the greatest sources of meaning in our lives comes from our being bound to other people, such as parents, partners, offspring, friends, and colleagues. True, not every aspect of private and public life is for everyone: Some people can be great children to their parents, great parents themselves, wonderful grandparents, amazing friends, and exceptional workers. However, not everyone is superhuman, nor does everyone have the opportunity to excel in every relationship they have. You may become a great parent and have a wonderful relationship with your children, but, if your own parents were nasty and abusive, you may not have a good relationship with them and understandably so. That said, most of us have the chance to foster relationships with a number of people in our lives, as well as with our culture, and these interactions could be among the most rewarding experiences we could hope for.

This is why finding the right balance between solitude and social interaction is the key to a healthy and fulfilling life. You can't always be by yourself, living like a prisoner in solitary confinement, or always be with other people, even if you're the most extroverted person in the world. Neither of the two extremes works. In both cases, you'll go mad. Solitude is internal self-reflection and exploration, while socializing is the external expression of the self that manifests itself in the presence of others. We become balanced and complete when we practice the two.

That said, since we're talking about Lone Wolves, the focus should be on seclusion and the inside of oneself. Moreover, it was established that solitude is largely ignored by most individuals and by contemporary culture. Balancing solitude and socializing to experience the best of both worlds is a different process for everyone, but all of us should try to tilt the scales in favor of spending time alone, especially Lone Wolves. To do that, you must know your desires, needs, and limits; this will make life easier for you and for those around you and will result in more fulfilling and fruitful relationships.

When you know what you want, you will be better able to communicate it, which is an essential skill if you want to boost the quality of your time spent with others. Although we know that most Lone Wolves aren't socially awkward, interacting with people properly and in a productive manner is a skill. Living in solitude for prolonged periods of time may make your social skills a little rusty, so it is important to keep them clean and well-oiled; this can be achieved by using those skills regularly. When you do that, you will be better equipped to explain your preferences to people, which will allow you to declutter your social life, putting the focus on the quality of your relationships, rather than their quantity.

Saying 'no' to people's invitations and advances is usually fine. This may not always be true when it comes to your closest relatives and friends, but it certainly is the case with people you don't know and whom you don't feel the need to engage with. However, you should make sure to do this in the most diplomatic way possible. Do not be rude! Being arrogant or too blunt in your refusals will offend many. Don't be a nasty piece of work. Moreover, people will treat you the way you treat them. So, be respectful and don't lie. Honesty goes a long way. You don't have to explain yourself at length every time you refuse someone's invitation or interest, but it's good to be specific.

If your more reserved demeanor doesn't work and if people can't see that you're not good at small talk—

because it's a waste of time—then make it plain that you have your boundaries. If someone fails to read the signs and keeps on pestering you, then you can say, "Hey, thank you, I'm flattered, but that's enough." You don't have to apologize, to say that you're weird, or ridicule yourself—though a dose of self-deprecation is always endearing and may help you in a situation like this. Just present your behavior as normal, because it is normal for you. In your eyes, the behavior of those who're always trying to make new friends in a very rushed and proactive way looks weird and strange. Explain that it all depends on one's perspective, and that any more substantial acquaintanceship with you takes time and effort, though such an investment doesn't guarantee closeness.

Naturally, you have to make some compromises with your time, if not for new people. then at least for friends and family. Maybe your dream day is to be alone all day long, to work on a project, read a good book, do some gardening, or all of these activities. Still, you can do all of these things and, in the evening, go out and visit your parents, or have dinner with some close friends in a nice restaurant. If you have the luxury of spending most of your time in solitude, some society won't kill you. You don't have to go to places you dislike, nor to new ones that you aren't certain about. You can go to larger parties if you're up for it, even just for a bit, trying to get the best of them and then leaving early, like a movie star. If you really dislike big gatherings, you can spend time with people individually or in pairs, which will make it easier to plan, coordinate, and manage them. You probably have a favorite cinema, theater, gallery, park, museum, hiking trails, restaurant, coffee shop, or even a bar or a nightclub that you like or at least find tolerable for a time. All these different venues are opportunities for some limited but vital and authentic human contact.

On the other hand, if you want to meet and get to know new people, but find doing it difficult and ineffective at parties or online, you will have to come up with an excuse for being with others. The secret is to find the appropriate setting. Join a book club; volunteer in a charity or cultural organization; start a team sport; do an evening course, etc. All of these can be enriching or healthy, but they will also give you the opportunity to socialize with a bunch of people on a regular basis while doing something that you both have an interest in. You will see them often and have something to talk about, which are the first two steps to getting to know someone better than just being introduced to them at a party with 50 people.

You can always retreat to your place of solitude, so go out on occasion and give the world the gift of your company. You will see that your human nature will demand that you find the balance between spending time alone and socializing. Or, as Seneca wrote (2008):

> It is… necessary to combine the two things, solitude and the crowd, and to have recourse to them alternately: the former will make us long for people, the latter for ourselves, and the one will be a cure for the other: our distaste for the crowd will be cured by solitude, our boredom with solitude by the crowd. (p. 137)

You, Your Social Circle, and Your Society

It is clear that "societal appreciation of solitude has been diminished, if not destroyed, in contemporary society," which is a tragedy because "[i]t contributes to the health of individuals, groups, and society" (Gordon, 2022, p. 1) itself.

We've explored many of the health benefits of solitude in previous chapters and will do more of that in the ones that follow. Here we can add that solitude enables us to play our parts better in society. When we're out in the world, we're many people. In psychological terms, we have different Personae—or masks—that we put on to play the varied parts required of us by circumstances. Depending on the setting, a man may be a son, a husband, a father, a grandfather, a friend, a lover, a distant acquaintance, a colleague, a plumber, a fashion model, a biologist, a public speaker, an employee, an employer, and so on. Sometimes we play only one role at a time, but at others we have to wear a few masks simultaneously. The only time when we don't have to do this is when we are alone. When we are in solitude, we can take off all the masks, put them aside, and just be ourselves for a time. This period of absolute privacy and truth is the thing that grounds and balances us. It gives us the strength and ability to go back into the world and play all these roles that are unavoidable.

But society is not all bad for the individual. When one lives in seclusion, one is spared much of the information that flies around in the world, from TV sets, computers, phone screens, or mouths, to people's eyes and ears. Much of it is unnecessary detritus, and getting rid of it can strengthen your ability to concentrate and boost your productivity. Yet it may also result in ignorance about current affairs and some changes in the moods of society, making your ideas and knowledge, if not obsolete, then at least different. As we'll see soon, diversity of thought is of crucial importance. However, truth can be very complicated, and to achieve it, it's sometimes necessary to hear opposing views that, through debate, would give birth to a balanced and sober truth. Such different opinions can be found among others in the public square, be it literally or online. Society is a corrective, usually an unjust and despotic one. But a wise Lone Wolf knows how to maneuver between society's inadequate demands and see the morsels of value that they offer.

Solitude can also improve your social life and friendships. Being a Lone Wolf isn't about being alone every day forever. Seclusion is meant to be used in the cultivation of a deeper understanding of oneself and of those, whom one interacts with, albeit briefly.

You can't choose your parents, but you can—mostly—choose your friends and your intimate partners. When you step onto the path of the Lone Wolf, you realize how much of your past interactions were superficial and automatic; you were doing what was expected of you and were close to some people just because of circumstances. You see that you should look for better company, because many of the interactions with friends are more draining than recharging. Some of your friends are energy vampires, who pour out negativity. These are people in your life who don't have a good effect on you and probably don't mean you well. You don't need them. When you choose solitude, you create a greater relationship with yourself and are able to detox your life from people who are bad influences. After that detox, you can go back to those friends and family members who really value and listen to you. Do all you can for them and forget about or ignore the rest.

If you're a true Lone Wolf, you can allow yourself to be picky, because you are a priceless friendship asset. Very observant and possessing deep self-knowledge, Lone Wolves understand human nature and the ways social groups act and can see when people are dependent on others rather than themselves. It is as if they know something about others that those others aren't aware of themselves. Moreover, those who prefer solitude are great listeners, since they have better focus and are curious about the world. Whenever they are with someone—which is a rarity—it is an almost exotic experience for them, and they listen with care and understanding. The Lone Wolves are also appreciative. Whenever someone makes an effort with a gift, a card, a cooked meal, or simply a good conversation, the Lone Wolves are greatly impressed and thankful. This, together with being trustworthy, loyal, and not gossiping, makes them great friends.

Of course, the Lone Wolves should make an effort. Make sure that the beneficiaries of your rare social outings really appreciate the time you spend with them. You should not treat these minutes, hours, or days of being in someone's company as a duty. Instead, do your best to show them that they are special. Listen to them, have fun together, talk to them. Make your friends and family look forward to the hours they spend with you, rather than feel snubbed and offended by the infrequency and scarcity of these hours. Knowing that soon you will be back in your place of solitude, knowing that this is certainly something achievable.

And it is achievable precisely because you're a Lone Wolf. It is in human nature to always fail to live in the present moment, in this way failing to connect and appreciate the company of those around us. One of the greatest Lone Wolves of all time, the French writer Marcel Proust, explored this in his grand novel *In Search of Lost Time*. In it, he shows us how we always think about the past or imagine the future, never noticing the present and, therefore, never truly living. We, Lone Wolves, in the long hours we spend in our own company, have to acknowledge the present and live in it. This is one of our main distinguishing features, and it is a precious skill when it comes to bonding with others. We can deconstruct our social life and rebuild it in a new, better guise. Demolish the ugly, concrete block of apartments that is your past social life and raise a new, beautiful temple, a Pantheon of your closest and most precious people.

Achieving this through solitude will serve not only you and them, but also society as a whole. Cultures have always stigmatized seclusion, because they see it as a threat to their ways and, therefore, to their survival. And that is not entirely untrue, nor wholly bad. "The development of individuality is particularly important in democratic societies" (Gordon, 2022, p. 2), because individuality brings diversity of opinions and beliefs, as well as independence of thought and non-conformity. All of these are of fundamental importance to the proper and just functioning of every democratic society. Of course, no society is perfect. But there are those that are worse than others. Modern democratic cultures have their faults, but living under totalitarian rule is dangerous and, for many, unendurable. No real solitude is permitted in totalitarian states, because they don't permit any individuality, and individuality is born in solitude. Being able to be yourself and to think for yourself is the greatest threat to tyrants. It is also the first and most important step to healing a society. That step is taken in solitude.

Chapter 5:
The Perpetual Distraction of Social Media

The worst loneliness is to not be comfortable with yourself. – Mark Twain

Finally! The Loner sighed with relief. He was alone again.

He and the other two wolves had reached the ridge shortly before sundown, and, after they'd seen the route they should take, they thanked him and turned back to find their pack and guide them over the mountain.

The Loner had enjoyed their company for most of the time they spent together and was excited to hear some news about the pack, as well as some other matters, like the fate of one of the old oak trees in the southern part of the forest that was struck by lightning, the newly arrived family of bears from the neighboring mountain, and the raising of a new village on the western edge of the beech forest.

Yet soon, this unending stream of new information started to bore him and he was reminded of everything that he despised about being in a pack. The constant twaddle of smells, movements, and sounds had been overwhelming to him and often pushed him to seek opportunities for seclusion. Even when he was one of the pack, he would take long walks by himself in the woods and try not to think about his brothers and sisters, their interests, desires, and fears. But he failed in most of these attempts, because their smells were all around him: Members of the pack would have marked their presence in this bush, or under that tree, or in that clearing. The Loner-to-be could not help himself but check them and then leave his own message. And, of course, there were the scent memories of all the other animals that reminded him of their presence, strengths, and vulnerabilities.

Although much of this information was interesting and often helped him survive, it was mostly too much for him to handle. He felt as if this following of unimportant trails and the belief that he had to leave his own was distracting him from what really mattered, which was the exploration of himself and the world beyond the pack. Even when he left his brothers and sisters, he continued to follow their scent for a long time, and breaking free of it took enormous effort and self-determination.

The company of the two scout wolves was but a small taste of what he had left behind, but it was more than enough for the Loner. Appreciating the silence, he started his descent down the path between rocks and gnarled trees, the sky above him darkening and revealing the first stars…

The New Chains of Social Media

Technology is a tool, and like every tool, it is inherently neither good nor bad. It can be used for many good things, as well as for doing wrong things. Modern technology, specific devices like computers, tablets, and smartphones, as well as the many applications they offer, especially social media ones, can be beneficial. These things, however, not only give, they also take and do harm. They are addictive and it can easily be argued that they have taken over our lives. Many, if not most of us, have "become eerily dependent upon technology," using it from the moment we wake up to when we fall asleep and allowing "[w]ork, play, companionship, dating, and love" (Gordon, 2022, p. 4) to be entangled and dependent on technology. On average, we lose about 100 hours each month playing games, surfing the internet, or engaging with social media. "That adds up to 11 years of an average lifetime" (Gordon, 2022, p. 4)!

Just imagine this: If you're like most people, you will waste 11 years of your life doing mostly useless, fruitless, and indeed harmful activities on your phone or laptop. Remember how short and uncertain our lives are and then let that sink in.

One of the many things that this use—or abuse—of new technology and social media has taken from us is solitude. It gives us the illusion that we always have the option to avoid being alone. Unlike in the past, when people could enjoy or have to endure long periods of seclusion, people today check their phones at every opportunity—be it appropriate or inappropriate—and more often than not have their headphones on, listening to music, podcasts, or something else that chases away their own thoughts. It is as if modern people have lost the ability to be with themselves and face their fears, desires, and ideas. Whenever left alone, and confusing solitude with being lonely, they fear the advent of loneliness and anxiously reach for the smartphone, hoping that the flashing images on its screen will distract them from what they perceive as their misery.

There is no respite from this. People grab their phones the moment they open their eyes and often fall asleep while staring at the screen. They even take them to the bathroom! It is as if everything depends on these devices. Studies have shown that young people would prefer "to endure the unpleasantness of a[n electric] shock to the experience of sitting quietly with their thoughts" (Alter, 2018, p. 169) and without their phones. "[S]olitude requires purposeful disconnection" (Gordon, 2022, p. 1), yet many seem unable, or at least unwilling to pursue it.

Destruction of Bodies and Minds

Solitude should be pursued, because this internet and device addiction and the resulting deficiency in time spent alone have serious and permanent health consequences. Even in the 1980s, way before the rise of social media, it was believed that being by yourself is "particularly stressful for members of technologically advanced societies, who have been trained to believe that aloneness is to be avoided and who therefore are relatively unprepared for its effects" (Long & Averill, 2003, p. 40) and, as a consequence, oblivious to its many benefits. If that was the case before the invention of the smartphone and the subtle algorithms behind most social media applications that have been created with the purpose of being more addictive, then how bad is it now?

It is very bad indeed. Internet addiction "leads to a disruption in sleep patterns, work productivity, daily routines, and social life" (Amichai-Hamburger & Schneider, 2014, p. 327), and the marriage between smartphones and social media has destroyed all balance and self-control in many people. Phones distract us even with their presence, because they remind us of the world outside and all the distractions they offer. There is even a new word, 'nomophobia,' abbreviated from "no-mobile-phobia," that "describes the fear of being without one's mobile phone" (Gordon, 2022, p. 4). There are people, especially among the young, who would rather suffer physical injury, than allow their phones to be broken.

This is enabled by the zeitgeist, while at the same time fueling that same zeitgeist. The contemporary self wants to be seen, to be known, to shine. It wants to be in the camera lens, to be on pictures and posts that their relatives, friends, acquaintances, and even people who it has never met like and comment under. The contemporary self wants to be visible and recognized, to become either celebrated or at least widely known. It seeks people's validation and is terrified of anonymity. Being unknown is an abomination; in the eyes of the spirit of the age, it means that you have no worth.

Social media is a way to avoid this, either by presenting your life as wonderful and positive, or by painting yourself as a poor victim that deserves compassion and help. But these avatars are illusions; people are more complex than what they present on social media platforms that take advantage of the human need for self-expression and presentation. People see these unrealistic representations of others and, being mimetic creatures, try to emulate them in one way or another, thus perpetuating the life of social media and creating their own digital prison. Fooled into thinking that what is being promoted on social media is authentic individuality, but is actually sameness and lies, we throw ourselves into a swamp of no genuine connection with others, destroy our solitude, and become unable to connect even to ourselves.

Few can tolerate utter and perpetual solitude, yet we all need some time alone. "[T]oo many fail to comprehend the risks of constant connectedness, whether physical or virtual," not realizing that the constant exposure to the manic atmosphere of social media "causes the adrenal gland to increase production of cortisol and adrenaline" (Gordon, 2022, p. 3). These are stress hormones, the prolonged effects of which can lead to depression, impair cognitive capacities, and even alter our brain structure—for the worse.

Social media overuse destroys both our social lives and the time we can spend in solitude, harming our health on every level. It is obvious that device addiction results in problems with our eyes, ears, and posture, but there are other, more insidious effects. Thanks to smartphones, tablets, and e-readers, chronic sleep deprivation has become a new, largely unaddressed pandemic. Troubled sleep may sound like a minor problem to some, but those don't realize that chronic sleep deprivation is at the root of health problems of all kinds, such as heart, lung, and kidney disease; anorexia and obesity; depression; weakened immune system; diabetes; and some forms of cancer.

Device and social media addiction hurt many of us, but the most affected are those who are unable to enjoy solitude in the first place—the lonely. If a "person's solitude-related beliefs and memories result in anxiety... Then she or he will likely retreat into loneliness or... Into the sociality (or pseudo-sociality) of mass media or communication technology" (Long & Averill, 2003, p. 40). It is true that social media, when used in a sober and controlled manner, can help socially anxious individuals reconnect with society and themselves. However, usually the opposite happens: Lonely people look for shelter online, but create a negative feedback loop, imprisoning themselves in social media, unable to connect with the outside world nor to hear their own thoughts. This is the "internet paradox," which demonstrates "that what was supposed to help build and maintain social contact is actually doing the opposite" (Amichai-Hamburger & Schneider, 2014, p. 320).

That said, even if you're a Lone Wolf and love and think that you have mastered solitude, social media overuse may creep into your life, eat away at your authentic alone-time and make you lose focus on what really matters. You may be affected by the tempting nature of the world that social media presents and, feeling that you're missing out on something, you may sacrifice your valuable and limited time on the altar of modern technology. You won't even notice how your blessed solitude has morphed into accursed loneliness. This state of being alone, but hating it and seeking escape through the superficial pleasures of the phone screen, is what we call "preoccupied solitude." It is the bane of productive concentration. "Distracted working, distracted driving, and distracted living all are hallmarks of our seeming insistence on technology-enabled multi-tasking" (Gordon, 2022, p. 4). Preoccupied solitude has created an attention deficit the human species has never seen before, hindering us from really doing or understanding anything properly.

Disconnect

Social media can be used in many beneficial ways. It does give the opportunity to connect and communicate in a world, in which the distances between friends and family are becoming ever greater. It is also a revolutionary way to promote and sell products or services and to learn about potential customers' preferences. Passive social media use, i.e., when one just scrolls down and consumes content, is mostly associated with low self-esteem and anxiety and only reinforces them. However, active use, i.e., when one posts and interacts with others, can boost one's self-esteem, if limited and done in a sober fashion.

That said, you will do better to limit your social media use to a minimum. Disconnect and embrace your solitude and all the benefits it brings!

You will find that achieving this will be surprisingly difficult. But don't be too hard on yourself. We're talking about an addiction, and coping with problems like this is never easy. Moreover, you must remember that this technological dependency is not a coincidence. It is "purposeful, pushed upon us not by altruism, but by the relentless pursuit of the dollar" (Gordon, 2022, p. 4). The Big Tech companies see enormous profit in making you addicted to their products. Behind every social media platform is a small army of very smart people, whose job is to make you obsessed with their product. "It is no surprise that many tech giants, including the late Steve Jobs… and Evan Williams, founder of Blogger, Twitter, and Medium, either severely limit or completely ban their children" (Gordon, 2022, p. 4) from using the very devices and applications they develop.

On top of that, the societal pressure to be part of the "online community" is enormous. Not being on Facebook, Instagram, or Twitter is seen at best as bizarre, and at worst as highly suspicious. Society wants us to be online, to be constantly available, and now whole new generations are growing up without realizing that there is another option. Furthermore, it was inevitable that one of the results of the COVID-19 pandemic and the forced isolation that it threw us all into would be the excessive usage of social media and the consequent loss of solitude.

And yet, we can win the battle! Solitude should and can be saved. We can choose to be alone and achieve it if we put our minds to it. Leaving the company of others and putting down or even switching off our devices is more than doable. Say no to the cultural pressure. Reclaim your privacy and silence. Resist!

You can achieve solitude through conscious effort. Doing a social detox from people that shouldn't be in your life is a great idea; we should also normalize the act of social media detox. Make the effort. Be more disciplined. Put down your phone. Delete profiles and applications. Leave your phone in another room. Have a regime and keep it: Use your phone only for an hour or two a day—mute it. Take long walks in nature without it and without headphones. Forget about the digital—focus on the physical and the spiritual.

When you do these things, you must remember your closest family members and friends. Disappearing from social media and not responding to messages and calls may offend many; it will also worry some. If your family and closest friends can't reach you for a day or two because you've decided to turn off your phone and haven't told them, they will start to spin all kinds of scary scenarios in their heads and may even call the police if you fail to reach you via other means. Tell your family and friends that you're disconnecting and come up with a way they can reach you in an emergency. You can mute all notifications on your phone except the calls and leave it somewhere in your home, where it'll be out of sight but in earshot.

I used to be one of the millions addicted to social media. Yet I resisted and managed to put that dependency behind me. If I could do it, so can you. Disconnect. Embrace solitude and silence and see how quickly you will find a new path that will lead you to a state of deep self-knowledge and may even be the beginning of a profound spiritual awakening.

Chapter 6:

Silent Meditation, Spiritual Self-Discovery, and the Secret to Self-Actualization

> *The more powerful and original a mind, the more it will incline towards the religion of solitude.* —Aldous Huxley

Soon, a dense pine forest overcame the rocky slope of the mountain. The Loner paused before it. The trees were tall and ancient; the forest was quiet and dark; there was no wind, and not a twig moved.

The Loner loved this wood. When he had left the pack, all this time ago, he came to this side of the mountain, wanting to escape far away from everything he had known. Although a predator and a strong one at that, going into these woods for the first time was scary even for him. They were vast, dark, and labyrinthine, and one couldn't know what to expect from behind the trees. When he went in for the first time, this forest made him see what being truly alone meant. Submerged in total silence and isolation, he had to make a choice. He had to answer the questions:

"Do I continue, or do I go back? Do I have what it takes to make it on my own? Do I have the guts to see myself as I truly am and to accept my nature?"

The answer was 'yes.' The Loner was brave enough. He went into the woods, confronted himself, and his eyes were opened.

He stepped among the trees once again. The sky had darkened long ago, but even if it were noon, the branches above him were so thick and densely interlaced that still no light would've been allowed. The smell of pine sap filled his nostrils and exhilarated him. There were so many directions he could choose from. Instead, after he went in far enough to lose the starlight that came from behind him, he stopped.

The Loner wasn't necessarily tired, but he decided to rest for a while. He curled up on a pile of dry pine needles. He closed his eyes, though he did not fall asleep. He fell somewhere much deeper than sleep. Listening to the silence and calming his breathing, the wolf explored his body with his mind. Soon he would have to accept the fact that he was growing old. Yes, he was still strong and fast, but the joints in his hind legs were aching in ways he couldn't remember from his youth. He focused his thoughts on them, exploring the tension in his tendons and muscles until he soothed them.

He then went deeper than his body. The Loner went inside himself, feeling his sharp wants and fears. He saw all the trees, rocks, moss, wolves, and other animals he had ever seen and would ever see. Deep down in the cave of his being, he felt the ancient beast, the First Wolf, who was part of him. He could see, smell, and understand his own nature and that of the whole world...

Know Thyself

An individual can achieve genuine self-knowledge and acceptance only if they have regular access to solitude. "[S]olitude can be… a commitment to positive values and dimensions of reality that are more fully experienced alone" (Barbour, 2014, p. 570). When done voluntarily and at regular intervals, it amplifies the extraordinary in the world and in ourselves and makes us see things that we thought were mundane and common in new ways. Genuine solitude is the environment, where you are alone with yourself and have the chance to truly see your nature. If you practice authentic solitude and not the pseudo solitude of numbing social media, popular culture, or alcohol and substance abuse, then you will be alone with your mind, listening to your inner voice, and contemplating your internal landscape. You will have no other choice but to face up to your past, present, and visions of the future, to examine your character and choices, and see both the good and bad about yourself.

Acquiring such profound self-knowledge will enable you to accept yourself the way you are; it will bring you inner calmness and peace; it will bring you home to yourself. That said, this doesn't mean that you'll be content with your faults and that you won't have to self-improve. On the contrary. Oscar Wilde quipped that "[t]o love oneself is the beginning of a lifelong romance" (2003, p. 554). Self-knowledge is self-love. However, genuine love means wanting the best for the object of your love. It is recognizing the good and bad qualities of the person you value, understanding the reasons why they suffer or fail in certain things, and trying—with patience and compassion—to help them ameliorate their situation. Genuine Lone Wolves don't love themselves in an egoistic or narcissistic way. On the contrary, their self-love is kind, but also constructive, for it points them to bits of their character or life that can be improved and encourages them, much like a kind and calm parent.

Moreover, solitude will expand your knowledge beyond the self. It enables an attentiveness that is unattainable in the presence of others. At its best, authentic solitude "is not oriented toward escaping the world, but toward a different kind of participation in it, as made possible by disengagement from ordinary social interactions," and brings us to "an encounter with sources of meaning and truth beyond oneself" (Barbour, 2014, p. 571). It gives us the chance to attain profound wisdom.

Silent Meditation

A good way of easing your way into the deep forest of your being is through the ancient practice of meditation. A "means of maintaining psychological equilibrium in a stressful world" (Salmon & Matarese, 2014, p. 349), meditation will soothe your mind and present you with new possibilities for self-knowledge and fulfillment. Silent meditation, specifically, enables you to access the depths of your subconscious and to find new ways to spiritual enlightenment. Keeping you focused on your purpose and objectives, it will unleash your creativity, or help you develop one, in case you believe you aren't the creative type.

There are many types of meditation, but we can separate them into two main categories: Guided and silent. Guided meditation is when you meditate while being guided by an instructor, who tells you what to do and who may have decided to use some background atmospheric sounds or music. Silent meditation, as its name suggests, is done without an instructor, sounds, or music. A practice that is more than two millennia old, it emerged in India and then spread first across Asia and then the world.

In it, you sit still and in silence. You focus your attention on your breath, try to steady it, and then you become attentive to your body's experiences and signals, as well as to your inner world. The benefits of this can be enormous. You'll learn how to distance yourself from the negative aspects of life and move towards a better existence. You'll familiarize yourself with your body and see its discomforts and pains; you'll get to know your mind, even its darker and more frightening corners. Through focus and reflection, you may relieve some of your physical burdens and heal many of your mental sores. You will see that the things inside you are not something you should—or can—run away from, but aspects of yourself that ought to be addressed and that many can either be resolved or come to terms with. You will develop self-acceptance and realize that there is no point in wasting time and harming your health by tormenting yourself about things that you wish were different. In many cases, you will see that the situation is beyond your control, that you can't change the world and, therefore, that there is no point in stressing about it so much. You will find peace. In this respect, silent meditation can be very much like the philosophy of the ancient Greek Stoics.

You can practice silent meditation in different ways. You can do it by yourself, or in a group, and you can even start under the guidance of an instructor. If you're a novice, it'll be helpful to have someone initiate you into it. However, meditation is deeply personal and proper silence will eventually require silence and solitude. You can also choose the length of your sessions: You can do it for several minutes or for dozens of hours. Your inner world is vast, so there's much to explore in it, both on the surface and in its depths. Of course, reining in your thoughts and superfluous physical sensations and finding the pulse of your body and mind takes time, especially when you're a beginner. It is best, therefore, if you do it for more than a few minutes at a time. Shorter sessions are acceptable for busy and stressful periods in your life, when you can't get more substantial moments of seclusion. But strive for sessions that are at least half an hour or longer. Practice brings us closer to perfection. And beware: Many things, some of them dark, from your past and subconscious will emerge and may shock you. If there is a place that you think is too scary for you to go to, do so carefully or only after you gain more confidence.

But when you make silent meditation part of your routine, you will reap the rich rewards of your labor. It will help you clarify your role and purpose in life. It'll be your reward for being different. Most people go about their busy lives without thinking about or actively running away from the big questions of life, because they're scared of the possible answers. But you are not like them. You are a Lone Wolf and Lone Wolves are seekers, who are not afraid of exploring their inner world and of what they may discover in it. You want to know the truth and find the meaning of life. You read, observe, and investigate religions and philosophies. Silent meditation is one of your many tools that enables you to go beyond yourself and find the existential, the thing that is universal. Pure Being! It will help you to overcome your ego, clearing away the detritus of prejudices, fears, and unnecessary desires, allowing you to focus on what matters. It is a highly subjective process that can't be fully explained; it can only be experienced. Everyone has to walk their own path that leads them to a place of new perspectives, which is the key to higher levels of creativity.

Awaken Your Creativity

We all want to be more creative. Each of us can feel the potential that lays dormant in us, and knows that it gets unleashed through creative practices. Besides, who doesn't want to be a talented painter, a great writer, gifted musician, or an innovative scientist. Perhaps you already are one of those things and are looking for a way to boost your creative energy. Or, if your aim is not the heavens, maybe you want to be able to cook a great meal, to arrange your interior in an unconventional, yet beautiful way, or to come up with interesting ways of building a new table or cabinet.

It is true that some people are more creative than others—it's as if their minds are wired in ways different to those of most people, allowing them to see unconventional solutions to conventional problems. Creativity, however, needs nurturing; people who were born creative have to tend to their gift, and those who believe themselves to be more conventional can find and develop their creativity.

This happens in solitude. Time spent in solitude, away from anxieties and distractions, fosters creative thinking and boosts productivity. Children who are unable or haven't been taught how to be alone "fail to develop their creative talents because such development usually relies on solitary activities, such as practicing one's musical instrument or writing poetry in one's journal" (Long & Averill, 2003, p. 25). Lone Wolves "are able to spend their time in solitude constructively" (Bowker et al., 2017, p. 287) and often surprise themselves and the world with the things they come up with. This is not to say that they find the world uninteresting, nor that they aren't curious of what other creatives are doing. On the contrary, a truly creative person imbibes copious amounts of information and inspiration. However, creative people know that at some point they have to sacrifice the society of others in order to devote their time and mind to their work, which most of them regard not as a duty, but as a vocation. And vocations demand dedication and solitude.

The reason for this is that deeper creativity requires patience and effort. Great art and music may appear effortless to the uninitiated, but in reality it is the result of enormous learning, prolonged apprenticeship, consistent experimentation, many failures, strong will and discipline, and the ability to complete projects and not leave them half-finished. For three reasons, all of which require solitude.

First, to be creative, you need to be inspired. Inspiration, however, is something elusive. You may be one of those lucky few who have been inspired by God, or in whose ear one of the nine Muses whispers instructions, or whom the vibrations of the Universe guide towards a new and consequential achievement. If, on the other hand, you're more like the rest of us—and more like most of the great artists and writers—you can't wait for inspiration to arrive, for it may never do. True inspiration comes with work. It is the result of a process of discovery, trial and error, and being diligent, dedicated, and determined to succeed in completing a project. It demands time and allows no distractions. A painter may have to paint for eight hours to do one hour of proper work. This happens in solitude.

Second, creativity requires a safe space where failure is permitted. In this, it is very much like the concept of free thought. If you're not allowed to make mistakes, change your mind, and explore new ideas, you can't really think freely. This is why we need privacy: In the privacy of our own homes or heads, we can test certain ideas and beliefs, make embarrassing mistakes, and reach some conclusion that is more or less decent, which we can then present to the world. Similarly, if you want to write a book, paint a picture, compose a sonata, build a table, invent a new source of energy, or make a cake, you need a safe space, where you can make mistakes, fail utterly, start again, make new mistakes, try again, and, at some point, manage to create something that approximates your original vision and that you're happy with. This happens in solitude.

Third, creativity is about solving problems in unconventional ways. The problem may be everything. You may want to build furniture for your living room; find a cure for cancer; paint a masterpiece; make a beautiful dinner for your family; write an epic novel. In order to do that, you must look at your problem from all angles, until you find one that may serve your purpose. This can be done by focusing on your project and trying to work towards a solution. Another way is to do something else with your hands—something mechanical and repetitive like washing dishes, gardening, ironing, etc., while you allow your mind to roam and explore your problem. Both tactics yield great results. However, in order for them to work, your creative space should be free from distractions. This happens in solitude.

By embracing the Lone Wolf lifestyle, you embrace yourself, your potential, and the opportunity to unleash your creativity, which will aid you on your way towards self-actualization.

Beauty and Your Home

Another step towards finding equilibrium and deeper self-knowledge is making your home beautiful. Solitude is about spending time alone. Perhaps you live by yourself in an apartment or in a house, or you live with someone else and you get your solitary time when you close yourself in your bedroom, man cave, artist studio, or office. In either case, the space where you spend your alone time is of enormous importance, because it affects you; it sculpts your thoughts, emotions, and, consequently, your actions.

It is true that "[m]any famous solitaries have mastered bleak and difficult physical environments." However, "the person whose characteristics facilitate feelings of comfort and control over his or her particular surroundings is more likely to find solitude rewarding than the person prone to feeling at the mercy of that specific environment" (Long & Averill, 2003, p. 38). The capacity of our "visual system to process information about multiple objects at any given moment in time is limited" (McMains & Kastner, 2011, p. 587), and people who live in unhygienic and cluttered homes show higher levels of the stress hormone cortisol, which is "an indicator of chronic stress that has been linked with adverse health outcomes" (Saxbe & Repetti, 2009, p. 78). In other words, if the space you spend most time in is messy, dirty, cluttered, and ugly, it may cause you to develop feelings of anxiety, even descend into depression. It will destroy your authentic solitude, turn it into loneliness, and deny you any chance of true self-knowledge and full self-actualization.

This is why you must make your space of seclusion, be it a room or a whole house, as beautiful as you can. People need beauty. It is possible to survive in ugly surroundings, but you can't thrive in them. "[B]eauty is an ultimate value—something that we pursue for its own sake, and for the pursuit of which no further reason need be given;" it "should therefore be compared to truth and goodness, one member of a trio of ultimate values which justify our rational inclinations" (Scruton, 2011, p. 2). We need beauty in our homes. They are a reflection of who we are and, in turn, shape us into something else. If we want our minds and souls to be beautiful, we must surround ourselves with sources of beauty.

Yet the pursuit of beauty may seem like a scary task. Making the decision to transform your home into something beautiful is terrifying because it exposes you. It reveals your taste and aesthetics, which may be tacky, cheap, kitsch, or bland. But that's alright. We all have to start somewhere and make mistakes along the way. By reading, looking at pictures, and going to museums and galleries, you can educate yourself about interior design, color and texture combinations, light, and art. Beautify your home gradually. Start by decluttering and cleaning it. Then make one wall or room as handsome as you can. After that, you can focus on the rest.

Another reason to be timid about trying this is that there are so many ways to make your home beautiful that it may be difficult to choose one. We can separate them into two major categories: Minimalism and maximalism. Minimalism is about sparse, even Spartan interiors, while maximalism is about abundance, ornaments, and many colors. Both are legitimate, though the easier option for beginners is usually minimalism. In it, you strip your space to the bare essentials, throwing out—or selling or putting in storage—everything that you don't need and that overwhelms you. Of course, a minimal space doesn't have to be devoid of pleasing objects, colors, and textures. On the contrary, you can make the most exciting yet harmonious combinations of furniture, walls, and accessories. You do the same with the maximalist approach, only there you can turn your space into a cornucopia of beautiful objects, patterns, textures, colors, pieces of art, accessories, carpets, chairs, books etc.

The important thing for both extremes and for all options between them is for the space to be clean, ordered, and balanced. When you achieve this, your space will give you the calm and equilibrium you need; it will become the true harbor of your solitude.

Reconnect With Nature

The space you live in is of enormous importance for your mental well-being and the finding of a solitary path toward self-actualization. But no one can spend their whole life between four walls, no matter how beautiful they are. Remember, Lone Wolves don't suffer from severe social withdrawal like the Japanese *hikikomori*;

they do go out. And one of the most important things they must do when they're out is reconnect with nature.

During most of its existence, the human species lived close to, or literally in, the natural world. Our severance from it is a modern phenomenon that started to occur just a couple of centuries ago with the rise of the Industrial Revolution in the West, the consequent urbanization, and the exodus of people from villages and small towns to big cities. It is safe to say that most of these cities, and especially the parts for the poorer strata of urban societies, were not built for humans to live healthily and to thrive. They are densely populated, ugly conglomerates of concrete, glass, and steel, with severe forms, inhuman proportions, and few, if any, open spaces with grass, water, and trees. These areas feel more like dystopian prisons than places where one can build a home, create a family, or find peace, and many have even developed the so-called "sick building syndrome (SBS) [which] is a collection of [architectural and design] factors that can negatively affect physical [and mental] health in several ways" (Ghaffarianhoseini et al., 2018, p. 99). Living in places like this and never trying to leave them, even for a short period, brings death to both body and soul.

In contrast, being alone in nature improves both our physical and mental health, lifts our mood, and balances our emotions. It is no surprise that all of us have the innate desire to connect with nature—biophilia. "Healthy adults demonstrate significant cognitive gains after nature walks" (Berman et al., 2012, p. 300), such as clarity of thought and widening of the attention span. Attention fatigue and psychological stress accumulate in busy and ugly urban environments, while nature brings us "physiological relaxation, positive emotions, and recovery of attention-demanding cognitive performances" (Korpela & Staats, 2014, p. 351). Studies have found that being in a natural setting helps people with "experiencing relaxation and positive emotions, becoming able to clear their minds, getting things in perspective, and pouring out troubles" (Korpela & Staats, 2014, p. 352). Moreover, people "diagnosed with major depressive disorder (MDD) exhibited cognitive and affective improvements after walking in a natural setting... Even though participants were instructed prior to their walks to think about a painful negative experience" (Berman et al., 2012, p. 303).

Nature has such a positive effect on us not only because both the grandest of mountains and the tiniest of flowers can be stunningly beautiful, but also because, without realizing it, in nature we ingest and inhale benevolent microorganisms, negative ions, and phytoncides that reduce feelings of stress and increase our serotonin levels. In other words, in nature, we get high on both aesthetic and biological levels. Moreover, we are multisensory creatures and sensory contact with nature, beyond just looking at it, is a great way to reconnect to it. Touch, sound, smell, and taste can transport us to another world that is soothing, beautiful, inspiring, and far away from the overwhelming and crushing atmosphere of cities.

Go out in nature and contemplate it. When you're in a field, forest, mountain, park, or beach, you should focus on the present moment and the things you can see, smell, and touch. This is mindfulness. Look at leaves, touch them; see how the water rushes and how gnarled the roots of the trees are; listen to the song of the birds and crickets, to the way the grass whispers; touch the rough bark of the trees, the stones covered in velvety moss, the soft tips of the grass and herbs. Feast on their colors, smells, textures, and sounds. Become like the great Romantics—like Byron, Beethoven, and Goethe—who were in awe of nature. Let your soul and nature become one. Find the *anima mundi*, the soul of the world, in your encounter with the sublime beauty of nature, the beauty that is beyond human achievement and control.

Make regular trips to lakes, mountains, and forests. Exercise in green settings. If you can't go out in nature, be it because of your location, health, or financial situation, then go to parks, have a garden, or at least make sure that your window has an attractive natural view. You have potted plants and flowers. Buy or adopt a pet and take care of it and love it. Pets introduce the honesty and immediacy of nature into your home.

Having a pet is like inviting the spirit of nature into your sacred space. Apart from populating your home with animals and plants. You can also decorate it with good paintings and photographs of landscapes and seascapes; albeit only a half-measure, this is a reminder of the beautiful aspects of the world beyond your space of seclusion.

Of course, as you should be careful with your own subconscious, so should you be careful with nature, because it can be dangerous. Mother Nature gives birth, but she also kills; she is the benevolent mother, but can very easily turn into an Oedipal one, who wants to devour her child. Never ingest plants or minerals whose origin and effect you aren't certain, nor approach wild animals that may harm you. "The evidence suggests that the company of friends may enable people to experience restoration in nature without concerns for safety" (Korpela & Staats, 2014, p. 363), so if you go on a hike in an unfamiliar place, you might want to pause your solitude for a while and go with a good friend for safety's sake, at least for the first time.

"[E]very human being has a unique and mystical relationship to the wild world, and… The conscious discovery and cultivation of that relationship is at the core of true adulthood" (Plotkin, 2008, p. 3). Run away from the concrete and metallic ugliness and fast-paced hysterics of the world and its information overload. Look for woods, mountains, and lakes. In them, you will see yourself, for we are nature. Going out into nature is actually going home. It creates a sense of wholeness and helps us see the interbeing and interdependence in our world. Solitude in nature gives us the chance to reconnect with our biological and spiritual roots and enables us to see the truth and divine.

Spiritual Awakening

One of the chief reasons for the true Lone Wolf to pursue authentic solitude, at home, during meditation, and in nature, is the attainment of spiritual awakening. Solitude is particularly crucial if you want to walk the path of spirituality. It "helps certain people to understand and feel connected to the fundamental sources of meaning and value in their lives" (Barbour, 2014, p. 570). The experience of authentic solitude and the self-examination that comes with it is linked by many religious people "with a conception of God… While secular solitaries do not link their ultimate values to the divine or an institutional tradition" (Barbour, 2014, p. 570) and instead seek transcendent knowledge that surpasses human constructs.

Spiritual awakening achieved through solitude opens your mind to the truth about your and others' situation. The Lone Wolves who go through a spiritual awakening are enlightened and self-sufficient. They thrive in the wilderness of ideas and the subconscious and are attuned to the vibrations of the universe, the voice of God, or the wisdom of their innermost being. They build a strong sense of self that grounds them and solidifies them in the midst of the chaos of the world.

Defining spiritual awakening is difficult, but it can be described as a subjective process of enlightenment that enables the individual to transcend themselves and reach new heights of universal truth, knowledge, and being. It can be a lonely but deeply rewarding journey. Without such a moment or period of awakening, we remain chained to the mundane and the materialist and waste our lives without even realizing that we may take a more spiritual path.

Spiritual awakenings are different for everyone. They may occur early or later in life. One thing that they have in common is that they usually arrive without any notice that would've allowed the individual to plan and prepare. Spiritual awakening is the realization that the mundane and visible world can't be the source of true meaning and fulfillment in life. It is a process of self-ascension, in which the individual asks existential questions about suffering, love, good and evil, death, and the meaning of life. It is about fundamental truths. The beginning of a search for the divine, the sublime, even God, eventually asks these questions and reveals to you the purpose of existence.

The process can be triggered by anything. Often, major life events, usually drastic changes, such as death, tragedy, trauma, sickness, war, etc., will open your eyes and make you question everything. Alternatively, you may find yourself suffocated with a boring and uneventful life, and realize that what you have and are cannot be everything, that this superficial existence is not enough. Or maybe you are more open than others and your temperament enables you to see things as they are even without going through tragedies or torpor.

Whatever its origin, spiritual awakening begins with doubt. You start to question every approved narrative and try to reach the truth. Your soul starts to grow, to evolve, and become wiser. Taking the first steps on that path and asking these fundamental questions is a shattering experience, because it destroys all your preconceived notions about life and the world. It is difficult but also worth it, because it deconstructs your being and gives you the chance to reconstruct yourself in a better, truer way.

Going through a dark, tormenting period is inevitable. You are at your lowest point and your soul is being tested. It makes you feel exposed, vulnerable, and raw. You find yourself in the midst of a desolate landscape, a wilderness that you have to cross if you want to reach the place of ultimate enlightenment and spiritual maturity. It is a painful shedding of your old skin and the growth of a new and better one. A destruction of the old and the creation of something new and superior. Like the lifecycle of a phoenix, the inner fire erupts, destroys the old unnecessary flesh, and births a new and stronger body. It is an ancient, archetypal battle, after which you'll be rewarded.

Some of the signs that you're going through a spiritual awakening are: You feel isolated from the world and from everyone in it; you've been abandoned; you want the truth, to know the meaning of life; you feel you don't belong to this world; that world shocks you, fills you with despair; you don't have a tribe; small talk is not just shallow, it is torture; you see that people are wearing masks that hide their unhappiness; you know that you've been taught lies; you have no more illusions about society; things you previously found interesting or exciting are now dull and boring; you feel exhausted and lack motivation; you're filled with melancholy, anxiety, or depression; you've become more sensitive and feel that your life is false; everything looks superficial; you see patterns in human behavior and the world; you seek solitude and feel the need to reconnect with nature; you become more compassionate and empathetic and want authenticity; you feel abandoned by the divine; you see the truth about your past behavior and, reevaluating your old habits and choices, see your mistakes; your intuition is sharpend and you become more forgiving to those who're unenlightened; you love more and more strongly; you have vivid dreams; you become filled with curiosity and wonder that make you a visionary; you realize that you can be the creator of your own life and know that everything and everybody is connected! You may feel it even on a physiological level. Your eating habits may alter and, together with significant changes in your energy levels, this will affect your weight.

This makes it clear that spiritual awakenings are strange and intense experiences. They are like a descent into the Underworld, journeys through hell, and then climbing back to the world and its light, carrying new and unparalleled wisdom with you. It begins with feelings of unhappiness and being lost that open your eyes and make you see the world in a different way. This propels you to ask fundamental questions and to seek the meaning of life. You may find some answers and think that you have them! But you will realize that they're either not enough or that they're false. This will plunge you into darkness; you will be in hell, a monstrous abyss that will be your biggest test. This is the stage of spiritual awakening that breaks many and makes them go back to their mundane and false existence. However, through meditation, deeper self-exploration, and asking the right questions, you may find the path that leads to enlightenment!

This is a taxing, nonlinear process. It requires time and may not work out on the first attempt. Keep in mind that when you tell yourself that you're not ready, you may actually be ready, and that when you're confident, you're probably in for a shattering disappointment. But when the time comes, you will see that you're an ugly caterpillar. Then, on your journey, you'll become an even less attractive chrysalis, until you reach the place of awakening and enlightenment and transform into a beautiful butterfly. Spiritual awakening is an inner metamorphosis that purges you from all unnecessary and false beliefs. It is the search for a better, truer path. The process may happen slowly and take years, or it may come to you with the swiftness of a thunderbolt. The important thing is to keep at it; don't give up or remain stuck in one of its many stages. Keep going and you will reach that grand vision and the peace that can be yours.

My spiritual awakening came with me waking up to the reality of my own life. I started wondering why I was here in a situation that was far from pleasing. I felt unfulfilled and unhappy with my way of living. I started asking myself questions like: What brought me to this life? Am I destined to follow the grain and work a depressing job until I am 60 just so I don't have to pay 10–20% tax on my 401k like the rest? Why can't I listen to myself? What is my destiny? It was an existential crisis, but instead of allowing it to depress me or to make me nihilistic, I got exponentially motivated by the challenge before me and decided to make my life true, good, and beautiful. The process was slow and painful, but it made me appreciate life and all its struggles. It taught me that with spiritual awakening, you learn to ask the right questions, find the answers yourself, rethink your state of mind, and reconnect with yourself and your life in an extraordinary way that only you can experience.

So, be open and welcome your spiritual awakening. In all likelihood, if you're reading this book, you're probably either already enlightened or on the path towards it. Don't be afraid and be strong. This process will change you, but you won't be detached from the real world, nor will you lose your individuality. On the contrary, you will become the best version of yourself.

Self-Actualization

Most people suffer from a terrible disconnection from themselves. This should not be surprising, because looking within ourselves is scary. We are the greatest unknown, and the unknown is the terrifying void. We wear masks as our personae, to fool others but also to fool ourselves. Behind these masks is the shadow, our subconscious, which is bottomless and may hide everything. And all things frightening and evil are part of everything. Many people can't bear the knowledge of the things human beings—and therefore they themselves—are capable of, so they decide to run away from that knowledge and live in some illusory world.

But this cannot be sustained for long, because sooner or later, we will have to face that shadow. A tragedy or a drastic change will expose our nature to the world and to ourselves, and there will be no escape. So, instead of being like a false version of our essence, we can confront our nature and learn to love our true selves. This reconnecting with the Self happens in authentic solitude, for in it we can't run away. We see the unknown. We get to know and understand ourselves—both our good and bad sides.

This rare self-knowledge frees us and helps us on our way to self-actualization. The psychologist Abraham Maslow developed the pyramid theory of the hierarchy of needs, at the bottom of which are those who're concerned with base physiological wants, while at the top are the self-actualized people, who transcend the base and mundane, see their potential, and want to realize it to the fullest. "What a man can be, he must be," wrote Maslow, adding that "[a] musician must make music, an artist must paint, a poet must write, if he is to be ultimately at peace with himself" (Maslow & Stephens, 200, p. 1).

Every genuine Lone Wolf strives to become self-actualized, because in that state "[h]e becomes... More truly himself, more perfectly actualizing his potentialities, closer to the core of his Being, more fully human" (Gordon, 2022, p. 3). Self-actualization enables the Lone Wolf to do what they must do and to do it well.

Chapter 7:

Skyrocketing Your

Productivity

A creation of importance can only be produced when its author isolates himself, it is a child of solitude. –Johann Wolfgang von Goethe

The sky was beginning to lighten. Above his head, small patches of cool gray were visible between the thick branches of the pine trees. From their colors, he could say that the sunrise was yet to come.

Slowly, the Loner rose to his feet, yawned, and stretched first backward, then forward, giving all his muscles a good and refreshing pull. After shaking the pine needles off his fur, he sat down for a bit and licked his paws.

The wolf felt well rested. His long journey from yesterday and the time he spent in the company of the other two had exhausted him, though not so much his body, but his mind. He had spent most of the night meditating, exploring himself and his nature, roaming about the dark forests of his being, facing his desires and hungers, as well as his fears and hates. Having understood them, he went even deeper, beyond himself, into the depths of the earth, below pine needles, grass, and moss, below dirt, stone, and roots; into the dark of nature's truth that whispered wisdom into his ear, revealing to him the meaning of his and everyone and everything else's existence.

After that, he allowed himself several hours of sleep. Although not much, they were invigorating. He no longer felt like the old wolf of yesterday, but like a much younger and stronger beast, ready to face all the challenges that the mountain could throw at him. And that was important, because with this new day and that new environment, he had work to do.

The Lowner started his descent through the wood, and soon pine gave way to oak and beech. He knew that there should be a small spring nearby, and, after finding it by following the music of its waters, he drank his fill. Refreshed, he began his exploration.

He had spent much time on this side of the mountain, but that was long ago, and woods always change. No matter how well you think you know a forest, when you go back to it you'll always find surprises. Since the Loner intended to live here for a while, he had to reacquaint himself with the terrain and its inhabitants. He had to know everything of consequence about the forest and to mark his territory. This was a lot of work and took him a long time, but he was determined to finish most of it today.

First was the beech forest to the west, then the oak one to the east. They were followed by the great moraine river that was between them, which finished in another forest that was a mixture of many kinds of trees, though hazel predominated. The wolf even went to the very edge of the trees in several areas of the wood and saw the small villages and shepherd huts that had grown there like mushrooms. Humans were taking over the mountain!

After noting the villagers' positions and the rough number of their flocks, the Loner went back into the forests, where he explored certain trails and found a good number of safe places that he could use for hiding in emergencies, like horrible storms, the cold of winter, or in case he was wounded by a human or another animal.

While he was doing his tasks, he met an old owl whom he remembered from before, and a badger that was new to these parts as well. The owl told him much about the time he'd been on the other side of the mountain, gossiping about this animal and that, while the badger looked at him with suspicion and, quite understandably, made it clear that he had no interest in making friends with wolves.

"Suit yourself!" thought the Loner.

One of the important things that the owl told him about was a couple of rather aggressive bears who lived in a cave on the west side of the moraines. The wolf decided that this would be an area that he'd better avoid since he didn't like bears, especially angry ones.

By the time he finished his exploration, the sun was beginning its descent. He was happy with the important work he had done and allowed himself some rest. That was when he realized he was hungry. Luckily for him, after he lurked in some bushes for a while, his patience was rewarded by a hare who hopped closer to munch on some fresh grass, oblivious to the danger that was staring at him…

Lone Wolves and Success

Being a good team member is an important skill to have, and there are areas in which one cannot escape working with other people. Building a whole house by yourself would be a difficult thing to achieve, unless we're talking about a simple hut. Filming a movie and being its screenwriter, director, cinematographer, set and costume designer, music composer, actor, editor, and promoter would be a challenge and probably won't yield good results, unless you're making some experimental video for YouTube. Writing a ten-volume encyclopedia on world history requires expertise in countless areas, and one individual would need several lifetimes of studying and working to just scratch the surface of the material they need to know in order to complete the series. Fighting a whole army by yourself is a suicide mission unless you seek the glory that would be immortalized in epic songs.

Yes, there are many cases where working with people is not only unavoidable if you want to be productive, but preferable. That said, remembering the long list of Lone Wolves, who were the brightest scientists, writers, artists, and composers the world has ever seen, it becomes clear that many solitude-loving individuals are

115

talented, hard-working, and very productive. Indeed, there are Lone Wolves at the top of every area of science, thought, art, craft, even stagecraft!

The chaos of a group rarely results in an excellent product, let alone the best product that will end up being loved by many and will have a long life in human memory or application in people's lives. Dozens of creatives worked together in the writers' room that produced the TV series *The West Wing*—or any TV series for that matter. But Leo Tolstoy wrote *War and Peace* by himself, in the seclusion of his study, as did Marcel Proust in his *In Search of Lost Time*, or J. R. R. Tolkien in his *Lord of the Rings* trilogy. Teams of designers, engineers, and assistants work on the projects of almost all celebrated contemporary artists. However, Michelangelo Buonarroti locked himself in the Sistine Chapel and painted the greatest frescoed ceiling of all time. Rembrandt van Rijn spent hours by himself in his studio, painting his many self-portraits that are almost universally regarded as the most profound images of self-knowledge ever created. And Claude Monet spent his whole life in quiet contemplation of the world around him, which enabled him to develop his unique and revolutionary impressionist style and gave us a myriad of beautifully painted canvases. Hundreds of scientists and scholars debate complex ideas and try to find answers to important problems in universities and other scientific institutions. Yet Sir Isaac Newton had to isolate himself for months in a country house during the plague of 1665, which helped him develop his theory of Earth's gravity. Marie Curie, confined to her lab, devoted her life to—and gave her health to—her pioneering research on radioactivity. And Albert

Einstein spent his time alone with his notebooks and blackboard, doing the work that was necessary for his breakthrough and the development of the theory of relativity.

In other words, many Lone Wolves are successful and very productive, no matter their field of interest and expertise. Of course, success is something difficult to measure. It is clear that an author who has written ten books and all ten of them are bestsellers is a successful author. However, one can aim lower than this and still be a success. One may not want to be the most celebrated writer of all time, but just an excellent gardener, who produces enough vegetables and fruit for himself, his family, and his friends on an annual basis. One may want to be an excellent parent or child to their parents. Success can be measured on many different scales, and the Lone Wolves can excel on all of them.

Why?... Because of what authentic solitude gives them. It makes them self-sufficient and mentally resilient; they have to learn to be more flexible and to master new skills; they don't follow unreliable crowds but think for themselves; they acquire deeper knowledge about themselves and the world. Authentic solitude is a productive experience because it "both requires and fosters emotional and intellectual innovations" (Averill & Sundararajan, 2014, p. 100). Most importantly, quality time spent alone boosts productivity, because it gives you the chance to ignore distractions and concentrate fully on your task at hand. In authentic solitude, we don't waste our time on social media or other mind-numbing activities like consuming pop-culture and too much sport. It isolates us from all these superficially exciting things that bring death to our ability to focus. Our brains are not good at multitasking, so living in seclusion and being able to concentrate on one thing makes you faster and more productive.

Procrastination, Discipline, Focus

Like everyone else, the Lone Wolves are human. There are those among us who have an innate ability to focus and to be super productive. For most, excellence, originality, and productivity require lots of work and dedication. Most importantly, to boost your productivity, you have to learn how to avoid procrastinating, how to become more disciplined, and how to focus more on the task at hand.

Solving Procrastination

We've all done it, and yes, procrastination is torture. To procrastinate is to find yourself excuses and small, useless occupations that distract you from working towards achieving your objective. It is a manifestation of weak will, immaturity, and even laziness. It is when instead of working on your research paper, or doing your taxes, answering those work emails, fixing the leaking faucet, or cleaning the refrigerator, you would rather scroll down your Twitter feed, watch content on YouTube, look at pictures on Instagram, or play games on your phone.

Procrastination is an almost criminal waste of time. We are all born, live for a while, and then die. Our time on this earth is limited, terribly so. Moreover, we don't know exactly how long our lives will be. Something may happen, and the end may arrive next month, next week, or tomorrow. It may be later today! Of course, we should hope to live longer and do our best to keep ourselves fit and healthy, so that we'll have better chances to stick around for a while. That said, coming to terms with our fragility and finitude ought to make us realize that the time we have should not be wasted. It is inevitable that much, if not most, will be swallowed by annoying and mundane tasks, even by tragedies, but there will be bright moments of happiness, joy, wonder, and love peppered throughout the darkness of our existence like stars. The more time we save, the greater chance we have to use it for something that matters and that enriches our lives. Scrolling down on Twitter while you ruin your eyes and neck, and reading stupid tweets about someone's unsophisticated and often rather hysteric political views does not fall into that category. It distracts you from living your life to the fullest and from doing the things you should be doing.

Naturally, to do that, you need to be motivated. There has to be a reason for you to do something, and it has to be a good reason, otherwise, why do it? This doesn't mean that the task at hand is something interesting or pleasant. It might be a terrible chore or a very boring job. When faced with something complicated, difficult, and tedious, it is no surprise that most people would procrastinate and realize that this is exactly the time to dust the top shelf of their bookcase, which hasn't been cleaned for almost a decade. In cases such as these, you have to remind yourself why you have to do this. If you have to do your taxes but hate doing them, just remember that you will hate the consequences of not filing your tax return properly and on time even more. If you're doing a boring, soul-crushing job, remember why you're doing it. It is because you need money, and money is a tool you use to get things you want and need. (Hopefully, one of them will be a way out of a job like this.) If you should clean your home but hate doing it, remember that you want to feel clean, balanced, and calm, which you can't do in a place that is unhygienic, chaotic, and frankly depressing. If you have to study for a difficult exam, remember that you're doing it so that you'll gain a new skill or get a well-paying job.

Fix your eyes on the prize and don't wait for inspiration or the desire to complete a task, because they may never arrive. Just set a time for completing it and do it. You will be pleasantly surprised by the feelings of satisfaction and relief that will wash over you once you finish. Unpleasant tasks that make us procrastinate are burdens that weigh us down. The only way of shaking them off and feeling better is by doing them.

You can also give yourself additional rewards. Promise yourself that when you finish the paper, clean the house, fix the cabinet door, or do your taxes, you will watch the new video on your favorite YouTube channel, or have a walk in the park, or eat some chocolate ice cream. Use whatever works for you and start working, remembering that every step worth taking requires effort.

Being Disciplined

Lone Wolves may despise the authority of others and the constraints that they try to impose on them, but they appreciate their own ability to control themselves. In order to be effective in solitude, one has to be disciplined and have a strong work ethic. It all depends on you, because when you're a Lone Wolf there will be no one to tell you what to do and when. Lone Wolves are able to control their impulses, stop procrastinating, and actually do what needs to be done.

This makes them very efficient, and, as it happens, there are many people who like working with Lone Wolves or have them as employees, because they know that they're reliable, responsible, and full of integrity. They come on time, meet deadlines, are honest and polite, and acknowledge and fix their mistakes. Of course, solitary individuals are often bad at cooperation and teamwork. Forcing a more introverted person to work with others is a recipe for disaster for both them and the team. This is why, when working for somebody, it is best to give Lone Wolves clear tasks that they are solely responsible for.

However, their discipline shines in its full glory when they work for themselves. Then they are organized, determined, and productive, and they can be more focused than many others.

Becoming More Focused

The proper completion of any task or reaching any goal is almost impossible if you lack the necessary concentration. This is among the most important skills one can master, for without it we really can't do anything of significance and leave our lives to chance and the mercy or cruelty of others.

This skill is best developed early in life. One of the important ingredients for concocting it is solitude. Children and adolescents who are comfortable with being alone for long periods of time and don't distract themselves with devices and television strengthen their ability to focus. This gets reinforced when they are given art materials to draw with, Lego blocks to build things with, and books with good illustrations and exciting, though complex, stories.

If you're a Lone Wolf and have enjoyed solitude in your earlier years, and if you were the beneficiary of good parenting, then you're probably able to concentrate better than others. Yet not everyone is that lucky, or maybe you've come to value solitude later in life and still struggle with keeping your attention fixed on the tasks at hand. You can't turn the clock back and alter your early development, but developing and training your concentration skills late in life is perfectly achievable, though it does require dedication and discipline.

First things first: Modern technology and social media. Stop using them or at least limit their use as much as you can. As discussed in the previous chapter, the addiction to smartphones and social media has a staggeringly negative effect on almost every level of our physical and mental health. One of the first things that it takes from us is the ability to focus properly, limiting our attention span and making us unable to concentrate on something more substantial than a five-second-long Insta story. Do what you can to limit your use of these devices and their applications. Delete some of the social media apps; use website blockers; mute your phone and leave it in another room; limit your phone usage to just an hour or two a day, preferably for the evening when you're no longer active, but definitely not before you go to sleep. When you wake up, and before you go to bed you should meditate, do exercises, have a prayer, and read something interesting.

Reading is the next way to develop your concentration skills. You must create the habit of reading for several hours—at least two a day—without interruption. And you mustn't read just any book. Reading some badly written Young Adult or chick lit novel won't help your ability to focus. They are the literary equivalent of easy to ingest and unhealthy fast-food. Instead, you must challenge yourself with some serious literature. Books from the nineteenth and the beginning of the twentieth century are the best options for this task, because they have complicated plots, many vivid characters, and are written in baroque and rich styles. Read George Elliot's *Middlemarch*, Tolstoy's *Anna Karennina*, Dickens' *Great Expectations*, Stendhal's *The Red and the Black*, Dostyevski's *Brothers Karamazov*, Jane Austen's *Pride and Prejudice*, Balzac's *Father Goriot*, and many, many more. Literature's chief role is not to be good for the reader but to be exciting and well written. These great books are both these things, but they are also good for you, in the sense that they make the human mind more resilient, train it to seek and make logical connections and notice details, and extend the attention span. Their effect on us is the diametrical opposite of that of social media.

Another way to boost your concentration abilities and your general well-being is to create and keep a routine. This should be an important constant in your life that balances your biological clock and helps you manage your time in a healthier and more productive manner. It should contain at least six hours of good quality sleep, two or three proper meals, exercise, time for reading and relaxation, and, of course, for work, either in the sense of your job or some side project that you do for fun or for self-improvement. You should dedicate the most productive hours of your day to that work. When they are depends on whether you're a morning person or an evening one. Some Lone Wolves prefer to have their most productive alone time very early in the morning. There are writers who wake up at 4 am and write till noon, using the quiet of the morning. Others prefer to work till late at night. The important thing is to do it regularly and to have the required amount of sleep. That said, every new day begins with a load of creative energy that can be wasted very easily if one focuses on doing chores or doing something useless immediately after they wake up. Don't do that. Don't waste it on calls, emails, texts, or social media. If you're working on something important and creative, it would be wise to devote the first two or three hours after you wake up to it. You'll be shocked by the rise in your productivity that this will bring you.

When you work, you must be organized. This doesn't mean that every minute of your time should be dedicated to something, nor that there will be no room for flexibility. But you must have some plan and follow it, at least until it stops working, when you'll modify it. Good time management is essential, but it comes when you stop procrastinating. Of course, don't forget to give yourself breaks and the occasional reward when you complete particularly challenging parts of your task.

Just like your home is important for your physical and mental health, so is your work environment, which is consequential for your concentration and productivity. True, it's not the most important thing, and one must be able to work in challenging environments. But distractions and interruptions are the greatest enemies to good focus and productivity. If you like quiet, then work in a quiet place. If visual clutter overwhelms you, then work in a minimal space. If you like to have a hot beverage while working, then have one with you. Do everything you can to eliminate these distractions.

That said, it is important for every Lone Wolf to remember that those who will distract you most are those whom you love the most: your parents, grandparents, siblings, partner, children, best friends, even pets. These are the people—and animals—to whom it's difficult to say 'no.' Your task is to make them understand, in the most respectable and kind way possible, the importance of your solitude to you and your productivity. Set boundaries and tell them not to disturb you during certain hours, unless for real emergencies.

A good habit to develop that will clear your mind and focus it on what's important is keeping a journal. Write in a notebook every evening before you go to bed, outlining the events of the day, examining your failures and acknowledging your achievements. You don't need to write long, flamboyant diary entries like some Victorian lady; they can be simple and to the point. This habit puts things into perspective, making you see your situation with sober eyes and identify aspects of your timetable or work strategy that need improvement.

Monk Mode

One of the methods of boosting one's productivity that Lone Wolves can use more than others is working in the so-called Monk Mode. This is a period of time dedicated to intense work on a specific task. It is the utter commitment to achieving a goal that requires much discipline and enforced focus. Lone Wolves are those who can do this because it is a way of working that can happen only in isolation from other people and all distractions, and that requires significant self-reliance and knowledge.

In Monk Mode, you can do any task. You can prepare for an exam, train to run a marathon, write a book, quit smoking, or renovate your home. It stops you from procrastinating and wasting your time on meaningless activities that give you superficial short-term satisfaction and prevent you from focusing on your projects and long-term growth.

In its essence, Monk Mode is draconian self-discipline and control that results in impeccable time management, which leads to significant productivity. It is like fasting: Depending on your goal, it can be done for short periods or for the long term. In Monk Mode, you allocate a specific time frame for the completion of a specific task. Achieving that objective may take a week, two weeks, a month, a season, or even a year. During that time, you embrace seclusion, eliminate all distractions, work towards completing your task, doing it in manageable stages, track your progress, and keep a healthy routine. You must be ambitious and challenge yourself, while still having realistic expectations and leaving space for some flexibility and change of plans.

Monk Mode is what many of the great Lone Wolves we know of have used on their path to recognition. It is a strategy that has proven successful. It is intense and taxing on both the body and the mind, but it is doable because it's temporary. You can't be in Monk Mode your whole life; but you can do it for a while, then reward yourself with a break, a holiday, or even a day in people's society, and then you can go back to it, doing what every Lone Wolf can, which is get the job done!

Chapter 8:

The Six Pillars of Self-Sovereignty in a True Lone Wolf

> *The greatest thing in the world is to know how to belong to oneself.* –Michel de Montaigne

His belly full, the Loner continued his walk, but this time his pace was calm and steady. He was in no rush to go anywhere. The wolf knew the forest well enough, and soon it and its many inhabitants would learn enough about him to know that they should respect and avoid bothering him. They would see this strong, self-sufficient beast and realize that he must be exceptional; otherwise, he wouldn't have survived, let alone thrived by himself.

As the wolf walked beneath the canopy of beech branches, he remembered the many difficulties he had encountered on his path: How unbearable it had been to be with the others. The enormous bravery that was required to leave the pack. There had been moments when he feared he couldn't do it, both before he walked away and after. Moments of terrible doubt.

How, in the many days and nights of solitude and silence, he had to face his true self and accept it, even the parts of him that were weak, dark, or scary. How he had to tame himself and learn to be strong, never putting off what had to be done. He learned how to rely on himself. Sometimes it was easy, but it was often difficult. But he did it, and that gave him the confidence in himself that he needed to continue on his journey. He was going to become the glorious, independent beast he was meant to be.

The Loner reached a clearing in the forest. A small circle of grass was open to the sky. The wolf looked up. The heavens were dark, but less because of the advancing twilight and more because of the gray clouds that were gathering over the mountain ridge he had walked over the previous night.

Yes. It was going to rain. That was a good sign. A sign that he had made the right choice…

Self-Sovereignty

Titles and recognition have little allure for the Lone Wolves. After all, in one way or another, most solitary people are rebels. High social status and public rewards are given by society, and society is the thing that Lone Wolves try to keep their distance from and often disapprove of. If a Lone Wolf is famous, rich, successful, or of high rank, it is not because they sought these benefits; they are either the result of coincidence or were awarded to them for their extraordinary achievements that were forged in solitude. No one would have heard of Franz Kafka had he not written his books. Nobody would care about Nikola Tesla if he hadn't made his contribution to electrical engineering. No one would know about Paul Cézanne had he not painted his groundbreaking landscapes and still-lives. Lone Wolves are interested in self-development, creativity, and innovation, not in getting to the top of the social ladder.

Yet there is a realm where the Lone Wolf is king: The Self. They are sovereigns of their own being, following no one and leading themselves to heights that few will ever reach. Every Lone Wolf is a temple of confidence, self-sufficiency, and truth that rises above the rest on six sturdy pillars, rooted firmly in the fertile soil of authentic solitude.

First Pillar: Self-Discovery

Being a Lone Wolf is about possessing deep self-knowledge and understanding. You go on a journey of discovery inside yourself. You ask the question: Who am I? Why am I here? What are my core beliefs? My values? What do I *really* want? What do I *really* need? What are the things that comfort me and those that trouble me?

You examine yourself with courage and understanding, recognizing the bad forces inside you and taming them; embracing the good in you and augmenting it. You look behind your many personae, your masks, and see your naked soul. You start to see changes inside you, the subtle or grand shifts that your character goes through, and, consequently, you can see the trajectory of your destiny. You know this gives you the power to control your fate.

When you possess that self-knowledge, the world can't break you. You're strong. You fortify yourself and don't allow the world to change your true identity. You know how to care for yourself and what to aim at.

Second Pillar: Self-Acceptance

You must accept yourself. Look inside yourself with honesty and accept your nature. You will see that it's composed of both good and evil. You must neither shy away from the negative aspects of yourself nor focus all your worries on them. This is self-sabotage. Nor should you worship them: This will be your undoing.

Self-acceptance is about knowing that you aren't and cannot be perfect. You diagnose your condition and see where you can heal and improve. You take responsibility for your failures and mistakes and accept your limitations. This enables you to plan and take the necessary steps for your self-improvement. It is a process that takes time and effort, so don't be too hard on yourself.

On the contrary, congratulate yourself. Recognise your achievements and strengths and pat yourself on the back for them. When you see them, you will know what you're good at. It will also show you that you can be successful. It'll make you feel more comfortable with where you are and show you that, in time and with some effort, you will grow and reach new heights. It will show you that you're already on the path to self-sovereignty.

Third Pillar: Self-Management

The best resource you have is yourself. Every true Lone Wolf knows that. This means that in order to succeed, you must learn how to manage yourself well. You must train your will and become the very image of good discipline. Holding yourself accountable, keeping things in order, and developing good time management skills will set you free. It will bring you independence, for self-management is self-control, and we can achieve what we want only through being in control of ourselves and the impulses that get in our way. Self-management is what makes us effective.

You must know your limits because then you'll know how and how much to push yourself. Challenge yourself to become more productive, but don't get overwhelmed. Self-management is not about pushing yourself too hard, which will decrease your productivity, but just the right amount. You must find the right balance, otherwise you aren't in control and this will lead you to anxiety and burnout.

Know your priorities. When you keep your eyes fixed on the prize, you will discover how strong your will can be. Be clear and honest with yourself. The clearer and nobler your goal, the more control you will have over yourself.

Fourth Pillar: Self-Growth

Self-discovery, acceptance, and management pave the way to self-growth. The duty of every Lone Wolf is to become the best version of himself or herself. This cannot happen without profound self-knowledge and honesty. You must be self-critical, though don't be too harsh on yourself. Don't beat yourself down for your shortcomings or mistakes. Give yourself helpful, constructive criticism that will instruct you on how to act and improve. Examine your actions: Which of them work, which don't, and why? How can you improve your situation and performance?

Examine your habits; uproot the bad ones, keep the good ones, and adopt new positive patterns of behavior. You must always improve. Hear feedback and advice from others and decide which of them is helpful and which isn't. Develop a sense of curiosity and work on widening your attention span. Learn to accept failure, for it is an inevitable part of growth.

Your life is your responsibility. You can't rely on anyone else. You're accountable and have to do the right thing. This will make your personal life, career, and spirituality flourish.

Fifth Pillar: Self-Confidence

Confidence is a feedback loop. If you have it, it'll make you feel better and more confident. If you have it in small quantities, you'll lose the little you possess. Feeling self-confident is good for your mental health and for your performance in all aspects of life.

To gain confidence, stop comparing yourself to others, be it in real life or on social media or on TV. Compare yourself to what you used to be in the past. Are you in a better position or not? Making your life better today than it was last week is easier than it seems. Make small changes to your life and in no time it'll be staggeringly better. This will make you more self-confident.

Don't be envious. Don't covet what others have. They're probably unhappy and are just hiding it well. Life is not a competition. It's growth, and everyone grows or withers at their own pace. Celebrate others' success. Laugh at yourself! Focus on what you're good at and know your weak spots. You may be confident in one area of your life but not so much in another. That's fine. You can work on the latter areas and excel in the former. Be grateful for what you have and what you can do. Imagine your life without these things or skills, and you'll see how blessed you are. Be kind to yourself.

Work on your self-growth. The more you grow, the more confident you'll feel. Have realistic goals and grow step by step. Climb carefully and gradually; that way you won't fall. Weigh risks, but don't be afraid of taking them. Admit mistakes. Learn as much as you can and be open minded. That way, you'll begin to make the right decisions, which will make you trust your judgment and boost your self-confidence.

Sixth Pillar: Self-Reliance

One cannot be self-reliant if one isn't a sovereign individual, and sovereign individuals are only those who improve themselves and dare to think independently. Not following predetermined beliefs without dissecting them first and developing your own well-founded opinions and views are the most daring things an individual can do. Accepting your independence is accepting your independence, which makes you responsible for yourself and your actions. These independent views are born of solitary self-discovery, acceptance, and growth. They are the values you must follow.

You can be self-reliant as in being financially independent, or living by yourself, or even growing your own food and not relying on the complex supply system that our societies have developed. But there is a deeper level to it. Self-reliance is about self-acceptance and not being accepted by society. Your culture and community do not necessarily point you towards what is right and true. Finding these things requires inner work and self-knowledge. Society can give you options, but it does not create value. Be a contrarian and dare to think for yourself, however, don't do it for the sake of being a contrarian; instead, do it because you've really thought about things and have reached your own well-argumented conclusions; you have reached the truth.

When you know the truth, you won't need to be a sheep following the herd. Don't seek approval and don't be scared of rejection. Look bravely at tradition and societal demands and decide what really works and what doesn't. Neither your community nor any individual can tell you what is most important. You have to decide for yourself. This doesn't necessarily mean that your conclusion will differ from that of your culture. But it may.

Self-reliance is realizing that your happiness and meaning in life depend on you and you alone. It is also the force that enables you to pursue them.

Conclusion

Conversation enriches the understanding, but solitude is the school of genius. –Edward Gibbon

The first raindrops fell. They crashed on the leaves above the wolf and burst into smaller droplets, some of which landed on his muzzle. They were followed by more drops, cool and blissful.

Something happened inside the wolf. He felt more alive than ever before. At that moment, he was one with everything: He was one with the wolf pack he had left; with all the owls, bears, hare, deer, badgers, pheasants, boars, squirrels, ravens, and foxes; with the trees, brooks, and stones; with the sheep, the sheepdogs, and even with the humans; with the clouds and the sky above them. He was thankful for the flesh of all the animals that had nurtured his body and rejoiced in the thought that one day he would be nurturing the earth of the forest. He was one with nature, and that made him feel whole.

The Loner started running, at first not knowing where to. He just darted through the forest this way and that for a while, but soon his direction became clear. He ran up the slope to a place where big boulders formed something like an island that rose above the sea of trees. He climbed on top of it and looked around.

The rain was still soft, and he could see far away. He thought about the people beyond the trees, about all the animals who were hiding under branches and in burrows, about the pack that were probably just going over the mountain ridge.

For some reason, the Loner felt the need to howl; to raise his head towards the heavens and make a loud wolf proclamation; to share his wisdom with the world.

But he didn't. He kept silent. Not out of pride or meanness; were someone to ask him about his secret, he would share it gladly. But because Lone Wolves don't need to howl. They acknowledge their success quietly, in solitude.

A Last Defense of Solitude

The cultural bias against solitude is not only harmful to solitude-loving individuals and to those who find themselves in a situation of isolation and want to make it work for them, but it is also dangerous for society itself. The stigma of solitude creates a society that is not based on responsible, sovereign individuals but on group identity. People are scared of being alone and being themselves; they don't like or are scared of their own individuality, so they project a group identity onto themselves. Although this may bring them some comfort, it suffocates their true selves, never allowing them to blossom. It is also dangerous, because it breeds conflict: The identity of one group is in opposition to that of another, and clashes between them become inevitable, condemning individuals and their communities to unnecessary and avoidable suffering.

This makes the practicing of authentic solitude and walking the Lone Wolf Way moral imperatives. They create independent, responsible, thinking individuals who are the torchbearers of truth. Without such people, there could be no functioning moral society, for everything in life will be determined by dictatorial government, corporate, and sectarian directives.

The good thing is that opportunities for living in solitude abound. Loneliness is the great pandemic of our time. For those who aren't cut from the Lone Wolf cloth, living like this must be very difficult. But for those who are solitary-loving, it is a great chance to embrace their nature and realize their destiny. All they have to do is be honest with themselves. As Polonius says to his son in *Hamlet*, "to thine own self be true" (Shakespeare, 1603/2001, 1.3.78). If your life is that of a Lone Wolf, then be true to it. Walk that exciting and potent path with determination, strength, and dignity.

Thank You

Hello! My name David, the author of this book. I just wanted to give my thanks and appreciation to you; the amazing reader that has just read my first published book! I sincerely hope that this has helped you understand your true lone nature, and how you could use this for your own great purpose in life.

If you have received value from my work, would you be generous enough to leave an honest review for this book?

Thanks again.

References

Aletheia. (2016, October 12). *Spiritual awakening: 23 major signs and symptoms.* LonerWolf. https://lonerwolf.com/spiritual-awakening/

Aletheia. (2018, July 9). *How to embrace being a lone wolf and walk your own path.* LonerWolf. https://lonerwolf.com/lone-wolf/#h-what-is-a-lone-wolf

Aletheia. (2022, January 28). *Seven signs you're a free spirit.* LonerWolf. https://lonerwolf.com/free-spirit/#h-the-free-spirit-has-the-essence-of-a-wolf

Alter, A. L. (2018). *Irresistible: The rise of addictive technology and the business of keeping us hooked.* Penguin Books.

Amichai-Hamburger, Y. & Schneider, B. (2014). Loneliness and internet use. In C. Bowker and R. Coplan (Eds.), *The handbook of solitude: Psychological perspectives on social isolation, social withdrawal, and being alone* (1st ed., pp. 317-334). John Wiley & Sons, Ltd.

Aron, E. N., Aron, A., & Jagiellowicz, J. (2012). Sensory processing sensitivity. *Personality and Social*

Psychology Review, *16*(3), 262–282. https://doi.org/10.1177/1088868311434213

Averill, J. & Sundararajan, L. (2014). Experiences of solitude: Issues of assessment, theory, and culture. In C. Bowker and R. Coplan (Eds.), *The handbook of solitude: Psychological perspectives on social isolation, social withdrawal, and being alone* (1st ed., pp.). John Wiley & Sons, Ltd.

Bano, R. (2022, April 4). *What is monk mode? Monk mode benefits, strategies, and planning.* Simply Schedule Appointments.

https://simplyscheduleappointments.com/2022/04/04/monk-mode/

Barbour, J. (2014). A view from religious studies: Solitude and spirituality. In C. Bowker and R. Coplan (Eds.), *The handbook of solitude: Psychological perspectives on social isolation, social withdrawal, and being alone* (1st ed., pp. 557-571). John Wiley & Sons, Ltd.

Berman, M. G., Kross, E., Krpan, K. M., Askren, M. K., Burson, A., Deldin, P. J., Kaplan, S., Sherdell, L., Gotlib, I. H., & Jonides, J. (2012). Interacting with nature improves cognition and affect for individuals with depression. *Journal of Affective Disorders*, *140*(3), 300–305.

https://doi.org/10.1016/j.jad.2012.03.012

Bowker, J. C., Stotsky, M. T., & Etkin, R. G. (2017). How BIS/BAS and psycho-behavioral variables distinguish between social withdrawal subtypes during emerging adulthood. *Personality and Individual Differences, 119*(119), 283–288.

https://doi.org/10.1016/j.paid.2017.07.043

Brunton, P., Huxley, A., Sarton, M. & Schopenhauer, A. in Chang, L. (2006). *Wisdom for the soul: Five Millennia of prescriptions for spiritual healing.* Gnosophia Publishers.

Camus, A. in Sharpe, M., Kałuża, M. & Francev, P. (2020). *Brill's companion to Camus: Camus among the philosophers.* Brill.

Ciccarelli, D. (n.d.). *Silent meditation: How to quiet your mind with this ancient practice.* BlogRetreatGuru. Retrieved August 27, 2022, from:

https://blog.retreat.guru/silent-meditation

Crane, B. (2017, March 30). *The psychological benefits of being alone.* The Atlantic.

https://www.theatlantic.com/health/archive/2017/03/the-virtues-of-isolation/521100/

Durà-Vilà, G., & Leavey, G. (2017). Solitude among contemplative cloistered nuns and monks: Conceptualisation, coping and benefits of spiritually motivated solitude. *Mental Health, Religion & Culture, 20*(1), 45–60.

https://doi.org/10.1080/13674676.2017.1322049

Elobeid, N. (2020, January 19). *Single life: Solitude has actually improved my social life.* Solo Living.

https://wearesololiving.com/single-life-solitude-has-actually-improved-my-social-life/

Flowers, B. (2019, December 3). *Why lone wolves are the most successful?* Bryan Flowers.

https://bryan.flowers/2019/12/30/why-lone-wolves-are-the-most-successful/

Franco, L. S., Shanahan, D. F., & Fuller, R. A. (2017). A review of the benefits of nature experiences: More than meets the eye. *International Journal of Environmental Research and Public Health*, *14*(8), 864.

https://doi.org/10.3390/ijerph14080864

Garrett, N. (2022, April 20). *How the pandemic has changed the way we think about solitude and loneliness.* Literary Hub.

https://lithub.com/how-the-pandemic-has-changed-the-way-we-think-about-solitude-and-loneliness/

Ghaffarianhoseini, A., AlWaer, H., Omrany, H., Ghaffarianhoseini, A., Alalouch, C., Clements-Croome, D., & Tookey, J. (2018). Sick building syndrome: Are we doing enough? *Architectural Science Review*, *61*(3), 99–121.

https://doi.org/10.1080/00038628.2018.1461060

Gibbon, E. in Carnochan, W. B. (1987). *Gibbon's solitude: The inward world of the historian.* Stanford University Press.

Goethe, J. W. von in Spencer, B. (2012). *Sanity and solitude: Cogent ramblings of a lone aesthetic.* Authorhouse.

Gordon, M. (2022). Solitude and privacy: How technology is destroying our aloneness and why it matters. *Technology in Society, 68*, 1–7.

https://doi.org/10.1016/j.techsoc.2021.101858

Holland, K., & Raypole, C. (2021, November 9). *What is an introvert? Personality, characteristics, type, and more.* Healthline.

https://www.healthline.com/health/what-is-an-introvert

Kaartoluoma, J. (2016, March 14). *Balancing social time and solitude: Finding your golden ratio.* Tiny Buddha.

https://tinybuddha.com/blog/balancing-social-time-and-solitude-finding-your-golden-ratio/

Kirsten, C. (2022, August 26). *Deep spiritual awakening: 28 major signs, symptoms & what to know.* Typically Topical.

https://typicallytopical.com/spiritual-awakening-signs-symptoms/

Korpela, K. & Staats, H. (2014). The restorative qualities of being alone with nature. In C. Bowker and R. Coplan (Eds.), *The handbook of solitude: Psychological perspectives on social isolation, social withdrawal, and being alone* (1st ed., pp. 351-367). John Wiley & Sons, Ltd.

Larson, R. W. (1997). The emergence of solitude as a constructive domain of experience in early adolescence. *Child Development, 68*(1), 80. https://doi.org/10.2307/1131927

LeMind, A. (2020, June 18). *Eight powerful traits of a lone wolf personality*. LearningMind. https://www.learning-mind.com/lone-wolf-personality-test/

Long, C. R., & Averill, J. R. (2003). Solitude: An exploration of benefits of being alone. *Journal for the Theory of Social Behaviour, 33*(1), 21–44. https://doi.org/10.1111/1468-5914.00204

MacLeod, K. (2021, January 1). *What the pandemic has to teach us about cultivating a comfortable solitude*. The Star. https://www.thestar.com/life/relationships/advice/2021/01/01/what-the-pandemic-has-to-teach-us-about-cultivating-a-comfortable-solitude.html

Maslow, A. H., & Stephens, D. C. (2000). *The Maslow business reader*. Wiley.

Mayo, T. (2021, November 1). *Pandemic solitude was positive experience for many*. Neuroscience News. https://neurosciencenews.com/solitude-positive-wellbeing-19579/

McGee, G. (2018, November 24). *The art of solitude: The secret to self-actualization*. Fractal Enlightenment.

https://fractalenlightenment.com/47493/self-actualization/the-art-of-solitude-the-secret-to-self-actualization

McMains, S., & Kastner, S. (2011). Interactions of top-down and bottom-up mechanisms in human visual cortex. *The journal of neuroscience*, 31(2), 587-597.

https://doi.org/10.1523/JNEUROSCI.3766-10.2011

Monroe, M. in Rattiner, S. L. (2000). *Women's wit and wisdom: A book of quotations*. Dover Publications.

Montaigne, M. de in Zack, N. (2010). *The handy philosophy answer book*. Visible Ink Press.

Moore, C. (2019, April 15). *What is self-reliance and how to develop it?* Positive Psychology.

https://positivepsychology.com/self-reliance/

Morin, A. (2019). *Five ways to start boosting your self-confidence today*. Verywell Mind.

https://www.verywellmind.com/how-to-boost-your-self-confidence-4163098

Oppong, T. (2017, March 31). *The science of silence: How solitude enriches creative work*. Inc.

https://www.inc.com/thomas-oppong/the-science-of-silence-how-solitude-enriches-creative-work.html

Peterson, E. J. (2020, March 25). *Integrity and inner solitude: Emerson on self-reliance*. Elizabeth J. Peterson.

https://elizabethjpeterson.com/2020/03/integrity-and-inner-solitude-emerson-on-self-reliance/

Pluess, M., Assary, E., Lionetti, F., Lester, K. J., Krapohl, E., Aron, E. N., & Aron, A. (2018). Environmental sensitivity in children: Development of the highly Sensitive Child Scale and identification of sensitivity groups. *Developmental Psychology, 54*(1), 51–70.

https://doi.org/10.1037/dev0000406

Plotkin, B. (2008). *Nature and the human soul: Cultivating wholeness and community in a fragmented world*. New World Library.

Porter, J. (2015, October 16). *How solitude can change your brain in profound ways*. Fast Company.

https://www.fastcompany.com/3052061/how-solitude-can-change-your-brain-in-profound-ways?_ga=2.66334187.432041200.1661414315-1072730904.1661327567

Rampton, J. (2015, July 20). *23 of the most amazingly successful introverts in history*. Inc.

https://www.inc.com/john-rampton/23-amazingly-successful-introverts-throughout-history.html

Ravelo, L. (2022, July 5). *The truth about lone wolf personality: Why some thrive alone*. Creativity Mesh.

151

https://www.creativitymesh.com/lone-wolf-personality/

Rich, J. (2010, May 12). *Solitude for extroverts: Medicine for the weary soul*. HuffPost.

https://www.huffpost.com/entry/solitude-for-extroverts-m_b_569564

Salmon, P. & Matarese, S. (2014). Mindfulness meditation: Seeking solitude in community. In C. Bowker and R. Coplan (Eds.), *The handbook of solitude: Psychological perspectives on social isolation, social withdrawal, and being alone* (1st ed., pp. 335-350). John Wiley & Sons, Ltd.

Saxbe, D. E., & Repetti, R. (2009). No place like home: Home tours correlate with daily patterns of mood and cortisol. *Personality and social psychology bulletin*, 36(1), 71-81.

https://doi.org/10.1177/0146167209352864

Scruton, R. (2011). *Beauty: A very short introduction*. Oxford Univ Press.

Seneca. (2008). *Dialogues and essays*. Oxford University Press.

Shakespeare, W. (2011). *The Arden Shakespeare complete works*. R. Proudfoot, A. Thompson & D. S. Kastan (Eds.). Arden Shakespeare. (Original of *Hamlet, Prince of Denmark* published 1603)

Shukla, A. (2019a, May 13). *Biophilia: Sensory contact with nature can improve your overall well-being & mental health.* Cognition Today.

    https://cognitiontoday.com/biophilia-sensory-contact-with-nature-can-improve-your-overall-well-being-mental-health/

Shukla, A. (2019, August 14). *The effect of social media on mental health and well-being.* Cognition Today.

    https://cognitiontoday.com/effect-of-social-media-on-mental-health-well-being/

Shukla, A. (2020, January 29). *Social detoxing and solitude: Alone, lonely, or aloneliness?* Cognition Today.

    https://cognitiontoday.com/social-detoxing-and-solitude-alone-lonely-or-aloneliness/

Silverblatt, A., Smith, A., Miller, D., Smith, J., & Brown, N. (2014). *Media literacy: Keys to interpreting media messages.* Praeger, An Imprint Of ABC-Clio, Llc.

Storr, A. (1988). *Solitude: A return to the self.* Ballantine Books.

Understanding the lone wolf: Confident individualist social habits. (n.d.). 16personalities. Retrieved August 24, 2022, from:

    https://www.16personalities.com/articles/understanding-the-lone-wolf-confident-individualist-social-habits

Twain, M. in Purushothaman. (2014). *Quotes to remember.* Centre for Human Perfection.

Usher, K., Bhullar, N., & Jackson, D. (2020). Life in the pandemic: Social isolation and mental health. *Journal of Clinical Nursing, 29*(15-16). https://doi.org/10.1111/jocn.15290

Vivekananda, V. (2021, May 23). *Social interaction, solitude and social media.* Times of India Blog. https://timesofindia.indiatimes.com/readersblog/the-eighth-colour-of-rainbow/social-interaction-solitude-and-social-media-32431/

Wahl, D. C. (2017, January 16). *Spirituality, soul and solitude in nature.* Age of Awareness. https://medium.com/age-of-awareness/spirituality-soul-and-solitude-in-nature-9c0c4f87d5f

Zach. (2021, February 2). *Seven famous creatives who found inspiration in solitude.* Creative Enso. https://creativeenso.com/famous-creatives-who-found-inspiration-in-solitude/

Zelenski, J. et al. (2014). Introversion, solitude, and subjective well-being. In C. Bowker and R. Coplan (Eds.), *The handbook of solitude: Psychological perspectives on social isolation, social withdrawal, and being alone*(1st ed., pp. 184-201). John Wiley & Sons, Ltd.

Image References

Alcántara, A. (2022). *Man walking into the sea with a torch in his hand* [Image]. Pexels. https://www.pexels.com/photo/man-walking-into-the-sea-with-a-torch-in-his-hand-12121577/

Bonometti, T. (2018). *N/A* [Image]. Unsplash. https://unsplash.com/photos/dtfyRuKG7UY

Brianna. (2020). *N/A* [Image]. Unsplash. https://unsplash.com/photos/BTT5CpOi6mE

Bye, R. (2017). *N/A* [Image]. Unsplash. https://unsplash.com/photos/JvUVo08dndQ

Carstens-Peters, G. (2017). *N/A* [Image]. Unsplash. https://unsplash.com/photos/RLw-UC03Gwc

Cassolato, D. (2018). *N/A* [Image]. Pexels. https://www.pexels.com/photo/person-holding-string-lights-photo-818563/

Citto, M. (2022). *Buddhist monk meditating* [Image]. Unsplash. https://unsplash.com/photos/_brhl3cAfB4

CottonBro. (2020). *A man sketching on a white cardboard* [Image]. Pexels. https://www.pexels.com/photo/a-man-sketching-on-a-white-cardboard-3778850/

Dom J. (2017). *N/A* [Image]. Pexels.

155

https://www.pexels.com/photo/assorted-books-45717/

Glenn, K. (2017). *Sunseekers* [Image]. Unsplash. https://unsplash.com/photos/_PuoQvJx7pM

Grimmett, C. (2018). N/A [Image]. Unsplash. https://unsplash.com/photos/MQzZ3adT8HU

Houser, K. (2018). N/A [Image]. Unsplash. https://unsplash.com/photos/-Q_t4SCN8c4

Kurfeß, S. (2028). *Phone wallpaper* [Image]. Unsplash. https://unsplash.com/photos/6lcT2kRPvnI

Mikoto. (2019). N/A [Image]. Pexels. https://www.pexels.com/photo/photo-of-woman-using-mobile-phone-3367850/

Neel, A. (2019). *Man leaning on wooden table* [Image]. Pexels. https://www.pexels.com/photo/photo-of-man-leaning-on-wooden-table-3132388/

Nevidoma, T. (2018). N/A [Image]. Unsplash. https://unsplash.com/photos/i-5L8PW33TY

Scarpitti, D. (2014). *Hike in the woods* [Image]. Unsplash. https://unsplash.com/photos/eWBseWsTEpA

Steve. (2016). N/A [Image]. Pexels.

https://www.pexels.com/photo/brown-wolf-682375/

Trish H-C. (2019). *Part of ancient ruins in Jordan* [Image]. Unsplash. https://unsplash.com/photos/xkiKgHZt4yg

Vitorino, W. (2019). *N/A* [Image]. Pexels. https://www.pexels.com/photo/selective-focus-photography-of-turned-on-light-bulb-2177473/

Printed in Great Britain
by Amazon